POPE
AND THE
AUGUSTAN
STAGE

Stanford Studies
in Language and Literature, XVII

POPE

AND THE

AUGUSTAN STAGE

MALCOLM GOLDSTEIN

STANFORD UNIVERSITY PRESS
STANFORD, CALIFORNIA
MCMLVIII

STANFORD UNIVERSITY PRESS
STANFORD, CALIFORNIA

LONDON: OXFORD UNIVERSITY PRESS

© 1958 BY THE BOARD OF TRUSTEES OF THE
LELAND STANFORD JUNIOR UNIVERSITY

LIBRARY OF CONGRESS CATALOG CARD NUMBER: 58-10474

PRINTED IN THE UNITED STATES OF AMERICA

For My Mother and Father

PREFACE

IN preparing this study of Alexander Pope's theatrical relationships, I have had two objectives. The first was to draw together the abundant evidence that for Pope the theatre was a vital, influential, meaningful institution. In his poetry and prose, in the prefaces to plays of his friends and enemies, and in volumes of eighteenth-century correspondence, biography, and dramatic history, there is much to suggest that the stage in all its functions was one of Pope's strongest interests, to be honored, on the one hand, for its contributions to literature, and to be censured, on the other, for its frequent appeals to low taste. In the following pages Pope is discovered relaxing at Twickenham with a friend's manuscript, cornering a manager on behalf of an ambitious playwright, pushing forward in a sidebox to catch the pentameters of a tragedy, and in his poetry defending the literary theatre from the encroachments of pantomime. Unless this facet of his career receives due attention, Pope cannot be seen in full view.

The second objective was to demonstrate the appeal of early eighteenth-century drama to a man of great taste and intelligence. An analysis of Pope's response to the theatre of his age should help to illuminate a period in dramatic history now generally regarded as barren. From the modern outlook, it is seldom possible to agree with Pope's judgments, but, if the eighteenth-century theatre is to be appraised accurately, it is necessary to understand how he arrived at them.

I am not the first to give thought to Pope's love of the theatre. Only a few weeks after I undertook my work I discovered that a master's thesis titled *Alexander Pope and the Theatre* was submitted to the University of Chicago by Mr. J. R. L. Johnson in 1922. But on reading Mr. Johnson's paper, I found that my study would not duplicate it. Although the thesis con-

tains many facts which I also found, and which now appear
here and there in my first three chapters, it is too brief to provide a full interpretation of them. I do not, however, wish to
deny the excellence of Mr. Johnson's thesis within its range.

It is a pleasure to record my obligations to the many persons who have assisted me. I am indebted to the staffs of the
Columbia, Stanford, Princeton, Yale, University of California, University of Chicago, New York Public, William An-
drews Clark, and Henry E. Huntington libraries (particularly
to Miss Mary Isabel Fry of the Huntington). Although it is
a small return for their generosity, I should like to offer my
warmest thanks to Professor John Loftis, of Stanford; to Professors Henry K. Miller, Alan S. Downer, and Gerald E. Bentley of Princeton; to Professor Ronald S. Crane; to Professor
George Sherburn, for permission to read proof of his edition
of Pope's correspondence; and to Mr. James M. Osborn, for
permission to read the manuscript of his forthcoming edition
of Spence's *Anecdotes*. Above all, I am grateful for the un-
failing cooperation of Professors James L. Clifford, William
W. Appleton, and Maurice Valency of Columbia University,
under whose guidance the first version of this book was written. Especially I wish to thank Professor Clifford; what merit
this study may possess is largely due to his erudition, patience,
and cheerfulness.

For the benefit of the reader, the following general notes
are given. Wherever dates in my sources were written in accordance with the old practice which began the calendar year
on March 25, they have been altered to conform with the modern system. For the dates of theatrical performances I have
consulted Allardyce Nicoll, *A History of English Drama
1660–1900*, II (*Early Eighteenth Century Drama*). Names
of learned journals have been entered in notes by initials only,
as follows: *Modern Language Notes*: *MLN*; *Modern Language Quarterly*: *MLQ*; *Modern Philology*: *MP*; *Publications
of the Modern Language Association*: *PMLA*; *Review of English Studies*: *RES*.

CONTENTS

POPE
AND THE
AUGUSTAN
STAGE

I

A CAREER IN THE THEATRE

ON the evening of April 14, 1713, the Theatre Royal in
Drury Lane was filled to capacity by an expectant, restless
crowd. Joseph Addison's *Cato* was the play. So persistent had
been the flow of rumor around the town that the audience—
made up of the most famous and fashionable persons in London
—knew that this was to be no ordinary first night. Addison's
name alone guaranteed that much, whatever his play might turn
out to be; but gossip, despite the playwright's denials, had it that
Cato was propagandist material directed toward Addison's political rivals.

When the moment came for the performance to begin, an
actor in Roman dress stepped forward to read the Prologue.
"To wake the soul," he began,

> To wake the soul by tender strokes of art,
> To raise the genius, and to mend the heart;
> To make mankind, in conscious virtue bold,
> Live o'er each scene, and be what they behold:
> For this the Tragic Muse first trod the stage,
> Commanding tears to stream thro' ev'ry age;
> Tyrants no more their savage nature kept,
> And foes to virtue wonder'd how they wept.[1]

For a moment the statesman who had composed the play was
forgotten, and attention was fixed on the prologue-writer.
These words declaimed by Robert Wilks were the first ever
written by Alexander Pope for the professional theatre. His
reward, which he was embarrassed to accept, was the uncontrolled applause of the audience.

Pope was still a young man when he wrote the famous Prologue. With the *Pastorals*, the *Essay on Criticism*, *Windsor*

Forest, and many minor poems, he had already earned an unshakable reputation. That he should turn to the theatre in 1713 is less surprising than that he had not done so earlier. Throughout his life the state of the drama was one of his greatest concerns, and the theatre was an institution to which chance and predilection constantly drew him. From boyhood on he enjoyed the society of men who looked to the often ungodly stage of the late seventeenth and early eighteenth centuries for their daily bread. Now at twenty-five he took on some of their professional duties.

Probably the first of Pope's theatrical friends was the great actor Thomas Betterton, whom he knew from boyhood.[2] Although Betterton appears to have been the only actor who came into his life so early, it was not long before most of the important playwrights of the age found a place for him in their company. Of the four successive groups who became Pope's friends during his family's residence in Windsor Forest, near London, each included established dramatists. In the first was William Wycherley, that relic of Restoration grandeur who, by the time Pope came to know him after the turn of the century, was ending his days in declining health and in increasing eccentricity. The second group, made up of the other surviving wits of Dryden's day, included the universally popular William Congreve, who had given up the theatre with the failure of *The Way of the World* in 1700. Pope ultimately lost contact with these writers, although Congreve's name appears regularly in his correspondence. Among the third group, the Whig crowd at Button's coffee house, were Addison and Steele. But it was with the fourth set of friends, led by Jonathan Swift, that he was to be permanently associated, and in that set was John Gay, perhaps Pope's most cherished companion, with whom he shared the writing of two plays.

At the outset of his career, years before the collaborations with Gay, Pope entertained notions of writing tragedies and was often urged to do so by his friends. Late in life he told Joseph Spence that

When I was very young, I wrote something toward a tragedy, and afterwards an entire one. The latter was built on a very moving story in the Legend of St. Genevieve. After I had got acquainted with the town, I resolved never to write anything for the stage: though I was solicited by several of my friends to do so, and particularly by Betterton, who (among other things), would have had me turn my early Epic Poem into a tragedy.—I had taken such strong resolutions against anything of that kind, seeing how much everybody that did write for the stage, was obliged to subject themselves to the players and the town.[3]

Owen Ruffhead, Pope's early biographer, added a comedy to this list and remarked that Pope occupied himself with these matters between the ages of thirteen and fourteen.[4] While we cannot be certain of the subject of the unfinished tragedy, there are two possibilities. It may have been the "kind of play" Pope wrote at "about twelve" for performance by his schoolmates, perhaps in London before his family moved to Binfield. "It was," he told Spence, "a number of speeches from the Iliad, tacked together with verses of my own."[5] But it may have been that this early effort was a life of Timoleon, the Corinthian hero mentioned briefly in *The Temple of Fame*, for, according to Joseph Warton, "Our author himself attempted a tragedy on the story of Timoleon; but not satisfying himself; laid it aside."[6]

Obviously these plays were concocted from the materials readily available to the boy. The curriculum set by his schoolmasters and tutors at Twyford, at Deane's school in London, and at home in Binfield would have included Homer; and St. Genevieve was part of his Catholic heritage. Yet these well-known tales apparently could not hold his attention for long; undoubtedly other topics encountered in the educational process appealed more strongly.

Another suggestion that Pope try for the stage came from William Walsh, who was so impressed in 1706 by Pope's early pastorals that he advised him to construct a pastoral comedy. But this would not do, Pope decided, for such a work was ill-suited to the taste of the time.[7]

Pope's brief flurry among the Whig partisans, his third group of friends, drew him closer to the playhouse. It is possible, though uncertain, that in 1712 he wrote a libretto for Steele's series of concerts in York Buildings, where works by Dryden and Prior were also to be given. On the evidence of a request from Steele for some "words for music" and one letter from Pope to John Caryll on the subject, recent scholarship has assumed that the *Ode to Music on St. Cecilia's Day* was written for the occasion. But the matter unfortunately remains in doubt.[8]

Late in 1711 Henry Cromwell added still another plea that the young poet turn playwright:

Leave Elegy and Translation to the inferior Class, on whom the Muses only glance now and then like our Winter-Sun, and then leave 'em in the dark. Think on the Dignity of Tragedy, which is of the greater Poetry, as *Dennis* says, and foil him at his other weapon, as you have done in Criticism. Every one wonders that a Genius like yours will not support the sinking *Drama*; and Mr. *Wilks* (tho' I think his Talent is Comedy) has express'd a furious ambition to swell in your Buskins. . . . In vain wou'd I fire you by Interest or Ambition, when your mind is not susceptible of either; tho' your Authority (arising from the General esteem, like that of *Pompey*) must infallibly insure you of success . . .[9]

The letter is interesting for the oblique reference to Pope's incipient feud with John Dennis, which was soon to erupt violently in print. Finding no merit in Dennis's windy *Appius and Virginia*, a tragedy unreasonably manipulated for the sake of poetic justice, Pope scoffed at both author and play in the *Essay on Criticism*:

> But Appius reddens at each word you speak,
> And stares, tremendous, with a threat'ning eye,
> Like some fierce Tyrant of old tapestry.[10]
>
> (ll. 585–87)

But the notion that he might be able to beat Dennis at his own game was not stimulating enough. Presumably at Binfield, Pope was so entranced by Martha Blount that he replied to Cromwell in a good parody of the pathetic style in tragedy:

> Tell me, by all the melting joys of Love,
> By the warm Transports & entrancing Languors,
> By the soft Fannings of the wafting sheets,
> By the dear Trembling of the Bed of Bliss;
> By all these tender Adjurations tell me,
> —Am I not fit to write a Tragedy?

And wou'd not these Lines sound admirably in the Mouth of *Wilks*, especially if he humourd each period with his Leg, & stamp'd with just alacrity at the Cadences? But alas! what have I to do with *Jane Gray*? as long as Miss *Molly*, Miss *Betty*, or Miss *Patty* are in this World? Shall I write of *Beauties murder'd long ago*, when there are those at this instant that *murder me*? I'll e'en compose my own Tragedy, & the Poet shall appear in his own Person to move Compassion. 'Twill be far more effectual than *Bays* his entring with a Rope about his neck, and the World will own, there never was a more miserable Object brought upon the Stage.[11]

Three years later Charles Gildon reported that Pope was actually at work on a tragedy about Lady Jane Grey, but the play was written by Rowe, Pope's friend, and we may be reasonably sure that Pope had nothing to do with it.[12]

Such is the history of Pope's early association with the dramatist's art: a juvenile tragedy, two proposals declined, and a doubtful libretto. Not until 1713, when Addison appealed to him for assistance in readying the fateful *Cato*, did he become actively engaged.

The path that took Pope to Drury Lane in April 1713 was rough and long. It must be remembered, while one attempts to analyze Pope's feelings about the tragedy and its author, that only a few weeks before the play began its celebrated run he and Swift had had their first meeting. Addison could not have known that his young protégé was, like Swift, gradually becoming alienated from him. Before the break was final Pope put much work into the play, but not all of it the labor of love.

The history of the writing of this uniquely successful tragedy begins with Addison's years in residence at Magdalen College. When the young man left Oxford to make the grand tour in 1699, he took a rough draft of the manuscript with him. By the end of 1704, the year of his return, he had completed the first four acts. Colley Cibber, in the company of Steele, read the finished portion in the same year and was warmly enthusiastic. Addison wanted them to believe that he wrote the first four acts for his own amusement only, with no intention of staging them. After deriving what pleasure he could from the process of writing and from the compliments of his readers, he put his draft aside. Possibly he had some private doubts about its value, for neither Cibber nor Steele would have wished to offend Addison by dispraising it. But the manuscript did not long remain neglected; in February 1713 Addison took it up again.[13] A conjecture that the recent success of Ambrose Philips's *The Distrest Mother* moved him to take another look at his own play may not be wide of the mark. Philips's play made its first appearance on March 17, 1712, at Drury Lane, loudly heralded by the *Spectator*, and Addison, impressed by the triumph his periodical had helped to create, may have begun to remember his own tragedy. John Hughes, a Whig partisan friendly to both Addison and Pope, undertook to write the fifth act, but Addison, rejecting Hughes's work, decided to complete the play himself. At some undiscoverable but late period in the writing, "the love part . . . ," to use Pope's words of a later occasion, "was flung in after, to comply with the popular taste," and the tragedy was completed.[14]

From this time the vague wording of reports renders the sequence somewhat difficult to reconstruct. At least it is certain that Addison next took the play to Pope and other friends, including Lady Mary Wortley Montagu, for rigorous critical evaluation.[15] Protesting that "he never in the least designed it as a party-play," he asked Pope to show the tragedy to the Tory leaders Bolingbroke and Oxford.[16] If Pope wrote down his reactions for Addison, the paper has been lost. However, two sets of Pope's remarks on the *Cato*, one to Caryll and the other to Spence, are preserved. To Spence, Pope confided:

When Mr. Addison had finished his Cato, he brought it to me; desired to have my sincere opinion of it, and left it with me for three or four days. I gave him my opinion sincerely, which was, "that I thought he had better not act it, and that he would get reputation enough, by only printing it." This I said, as thinking the lines well written, but the piece not theatrical enough.—Sometime after Mr. Addison said; "That his own opinion was the same with mine; but that some particular friends of his, whom he could not disoblige, insisted on its being acted." And so it was, you know, with the greatest applause.[17]

The phrase "sometime after" suggests that Addison, unhappy with Pope's opinion, asked Lady Mary and others (Steele and

Cibber perhaps) merely to confirm his own judgment. Another possibility is that Addison let Pope read *Cato* after the "particular friends" had seen it, received Pope's disappointing reply, and then took the play back to Pope with a request for suggestions toward possible revisions. In either event, Addison, having now determined to take his drama out of the closet, did obtain further assistance from Pope. *Cato* thus became the first of many plays to which Pope lent his services as adviser.

The range of Pope's work on *Cato* cannot be deduced exactly, but it must have been extensive. Again the information is provided through Pope's conversations with Spence:

Mr. Addison would never alter any thing after a poem was once printed; and was ready to alter almost everything that was found fault with before.—I believe he did not leave a word unchanged, that I made a scruple against in his Cato.

To this Spence added, "The last line in that tragedy originally
'And oh, 'twas this that ended Cato's life.'
It was Mr. Pope who suggested the alteration as it stands at present." In a note Spence continued:

A passage was objected to by Mrs. Oldfield ⌈stiffens as he stands⌉ and Mr. Pope suggested the alteration to 'stiffens yet alive.'—'So the fair limpid stream' ⌈at the close of 'So where our wide Numidian'⌉ &c.— tautology, a frequent fault of Addison: more such faults in his Campaign than any one would easily imagine.[18]

Pope's letter to Caryll is all praise with not a word of doubt on the theatrical success of the tragedy:

I have lately had the entertainment of reading Mr. Addison's tragedy of *Cato*. The scene is Utica, and the time the last night of his life. It drew tears from me in several parts of the fourth and fifth acts, where the beauty of virtue appears so charming that I believe (if it comes upon the theatre) we shall enjoy that which Plato thought the greatest pleasure an exalted soul could be capable of, a view of virtue itself great in person, colour, and action. The emotion which the mind will feel from this character, and the sentiments of humanity which the distress of such a person as Cato will stir up in us, must necessarily fill an audience with so glorious a disposition, and so warm a love of virtue, that I question if any play has ever conduced so immediately to morals as this.[19]

The letter and the comments to Spence do not wholly agree, but in Pope's defense one may conjecture that he wrote to Caryll only after he had made suggestions to Addison and found them effective.

As the time grew short before the opening, factional excitement began to run high. It amused Swift, still friendly with Addison, to write home to Stella that he had attended a rehearsal and had watched the author directing his cast.[20] Looking forward to the performance, both Whigs and Tories expected something momentous. Steele, acting on Addison's request to insure a favorable audience, packed the house with well-disposed persons.[21] This was no novel procedure, for, as Pope commented, "An audience was laid for the Distressed Mother; and when they found it would do, it was practised again, yet more successfully for Cato."[22] But the alerted Tories were forming plans of their own.

All accounts of the evening agree that the responses of the audience were violent and that Pope's share in the proceedings was attended closely. George Berkeley, present that evening, wrote to Sir John Percival that the Tories hissed parts of the Prologue, "written by Mr. Pope, a Tory and even a Papist, being thought to savour of Whiggism . . ."[23] The Whigs thereupon responded with tremendous applause. Pope has given the fullest account of the occasion in a letter to Caryll of April 30, 1713:

Cato was not so much the wonder of Rome itself, in his days, as he is of Britain in ours; and tho' all the foolish industry possible has been used to make it a party play, yet what the author once said of another may be the most properly in the world applied to him on this occasion.

> Envy itself is dumb, in wonder lost,
> And factions strive, who shall applaud him most.

The numerous and violent claps of the Whig party on the one side of the theatre, were echoed back by the Tories on the other, while the author sweated behind the scenes with concern to find their applause proceeded more from the hand than the head. This was the case too of the prologue-writer, who was clapped into a staunch Whig, sore against his will, at almost every two lines. I believe you may have heard that, after all the applauses of the opposite faction, my Lord Bullingbrooke sent for Booth who played Cato, into the box, between one of the acts and presented him with 50 guineas; in acknowledgement (as he expressed it) for his defending the cause of liberty so well against a *perpetuall dictator*: the Whigs were unwilling to be distanced this way, as 'tis said, and therefore design a present to the said Cato very speedily; in the meantime they are getting ready as good a sentence as the former on their side. So betwixt them, it is probable that Cato (as Dr Garth expressed it) may have something to live upon, after he dies.

This play was published but this Munday and Mr. Lewis tells me it is not possible to convey it to you before Friday next. The town is so fond of it, that the orange wenches and fruit women in the Park offer the books at the side of the coaches, and the Prologue and Epilogue are cried about the streets by the common hawkers.

But of all the world none have been in so peculiar a manner enamoured with *Cato*, as a young gentleman of Oxford, who makes it the sole guide of all his actions, the subject of all his discourse; he dates everything from the first or third night, &c., of *Cato*: he goes out of town every day it is not played, and fell in love with Mrs. Oldfield for no other reason than because she acted Cato's daughter![24]

Notwithstanding those unbelievers among the Tories who took exception to his Prologue, the letter suggests that Pope had begun to identify himself with Tory interests. What he repeated of the gossip of the Whigs' gift to Booth reveals that he found nothing to admire in the gesture. As for the gift itself, Cibber relates that the actor Doggett, truly a "staunch Whig," and Wilks determined to bestow a sum upon Booth equal to that given by the Tories.[25]

Thus Whig and Tory made political capital of the play, and the sensation continued. *Cato* played an unprecedented twenty-five performances during the course of the calendar year and proved an astonishing success in Oxford when the Drury Lane troupe took it there.[26]

To echo Samuel Johnson on the play, "Of a work so much read, it is difficult to say anything new." Yet a glance at *Cato* through Pope's eyes may lead to a proper assessment of its popu-

larity, for he openly praised and blamed Addison as he saw fit.
To Caryll, it will be remembered, he declared that the fourth
and fifth acts, wherein "the beauty of virtue appears so charming," drew tears from him. Furthermore, he believed the play
would prove morally uplifting because of its sentimental and
emotional impact on the audience. Pathos, then, as developed
by the spectacle of the doomed hero, was the strength of the
play. The fact that Addison gave Cato no moment of self-
recognition, no opportunity to achieve the stature of a tragic
figure, apparently counted for nothing.

For many members of the audience the value of *Cato* lay
in its political significance, and such persons accepted it on
faith as literary art. What is known of the first performance
suggests that partisanship was the reason for the popularity of
the tragedy not only in 1713 but throughout the age. To a
limited extent such feelings account for Pope's original interest in it. He was no politician, but he was intelligent enough to
know from the start that *Cato* would figure in the Whig-Tory
controversy, and, in fact, he cooled toward the play very rapidly
once he was drawn into Swift's orbit.

Yet to certain others in the audience who cared nothing at
all for politics, *Cato* was still an artistic success. Those clamor-
ous throngs who kept the tragedy on the boards for succeeding
decades took delight in its "regular" construction and sentimentality. The continual play on the emotions as the characters move from joy to sadness was in *Cato* accompanied by a
code of stoicism and virtue. When these qualities were linked
to an essentially simple love story, the piece proved irresistible.
As a factor in the success of the play, the "love part" should
not be minimized, for many years later the plays of which Pope
himself approved failed for the lack of this touch of humanity
though they were as carefully designed in accordance with the
rules as *Cato*.

To Pope the love story in Addison's play was unacceptable.
"Virtue," "emotion," "humanity," and "distress" were the
words he used to describe the play to Caryll. Obviously he considered the Marcus-Lucia-Portius triangle no more than a sop
to popular taste. The discriminating few, himself included,
might take the rigorous neoclassical material undiluted by maud-

lin romance. He was a child of his age in appreciating regular tragedy buttressed by moral philosophy, but he displayed his essential hardheadedness in resisting the insidious attraction of eye-drowning romance, and his Prologue admonishes against it:

> Our author shuns by vulgar springs to move,
> The hero's glory, or the virgin's love;
> In pitying love we but our weakness show,
> And wild ambition well deserves its woe.
> Here tears shall flow from a more gen'rous cause
> Such tears, as Patriots shed for dying Laws . . .[27]
>
> (ll. 9–14)

Since prologues and epilogues were normally the last lines to be written for new plays, it is unlikely that Pope wrote the piece before the romantic underplot was added to the tragedy. This was probably an attempt to deflect attention of the audience from the love story.

Gradually, however, Pope's public attitude toward Addison's tragedy underwent revision. His letter to Caryll, previously quoted, concludes with some lines inspired by Mrs. Oldfield, who played Marcia, which bespeak a new and irreverent attitude:

> On CATO
>
> You ask why Damon does the College seek?
> 'Tis because Cato's not rehears'd this week:
> How long at Oxford then will Damon stay?
> Damon returns not till they Cato Play:
> Oldfield wants Damon—when will he be at her?
> Oh, not till Oldfield shall be Cato's Daughter:
> Why then if I can guess what may ensue,
> When Cato's clapp'd, Damon will be so too.[28]

Scholarship cannot determine whether this little poem is from Pope's pen or merely a popular squib which he thought might amuse his friend, but certainly it is full of the sense of robust, if not clean, fun often present in his unacknowledged verse, and his willingness to direct it to a sympathetic ear tells something about his changing view of Cato, for the abuse of its leading actress was bound to reflect on the prestige of the play. Possibly the poet lost patience with her over an unpleasant incident during rehearsals, such as the one previously cited. But quite apart from what harm the poem might conceivably have done to Mrs. Oldfield's reputation, it could scarcely have been composed in honor of the play.

Addison, however, probably did not hear of Pope's glee over the little poem, since so far as is known Pope passed it on only to Caryll. Nothing had yet occurred to mar the friendship of the poet and statesman. It is likely, in fact, that in 1713 Pope wrote a prologue to be spoken at a benefit honoring Tom D'Urfey at Addison's request. In his *Miscellanies* of December 1713, Steele published such a poem, "Written by several Hands." Pope included it in the *Miscellanies* of 1727, and scholars have usually attributed it to him despite his failure to acknowledge it. Probably the Prologue was composed for a performance of D'Urfey's *A Fond Husband: or, The Plotting Sisters*, revived in June through Addison's good offices. Pope, if indeed it was he, congratulated D'Urfey for inventing his own plots rather than adapting familiar ones:

> You modern Wits, should each Man bring his Claim,
> Have desperate Debentures on your Fame;
> And little wou'd be left you, I'm afraid,
> If all your Debts to *Greece* and *Rome* were paid.
> From his deep Fund our Author largely draws;
> Nor sinks his Credit lower than it was.[29]

(ll. 11–16)

Complaints on the score of unoriginality were almost habitual with Pope; he raised the same issue in the Prologue to *Cato* and was to do so repeatedly in the *Dunciad*.

Meanwhile, the wars of *Cato* were under way. Early in July 1713, John Dennis delivered himself of several pages of wrathful fulminations on the tragedy. Remaining unmoved while an enthusiastic public acclaimed Addison, Dennis found the work faulty and uninspiring. Not only did it violate the rules—chiefly, Dennis seems to have believed, by cramming too much into the narrow confines of the unities—but when examined closely the total effect of the play opposed Addison's intentions. The difficulty lay, Dennis reasoned, in Addison's

attempt to defend liberty with such a plot as the life of Cato
afforded, for the virtuous and dedicated man did not triumph
over his opposition.[30] Had Dennis controlled his heat and made
his sense of outrage less evident, he might have been credited
with a greater achievement. But his fury and stubbornness obscured for his contemporaries the depth of his insights.

Dennis soon suffered a hearty counterattack for his pains.
Within three weeks of the publication of his remarks, a pamphlet appeared titled *The Narrative of Dr. Robert Norris*. The
piece purported to be an account by a well-known handler of
lunatics of his visit to a difficult patient, who is actually Dennis.
While the extent of Pope's connection with the pamphlet cannot be defined, it is certain that he was in some way behind it.
A legend has developed that Pope, hearing of Dennis's critique
of *Cato*, persuaded Bernard Lintot to publish it that he might
later lampoon the critic. Dennis himself thought so, and he
eventually set down his opinion in the libelous *True Character
of Mr. Pope* (1716).[31] But no evidence exists to support this
charge. The *Remarks on Cato* inspired *The Narrative of Dr.
Robert Norris*, however, because in the *Narrative* Dennis is caricatured as a man put out of his senses by Addison's play.

The *Narrative*, in brief, is that Dr. Norris received a call
from an old woman-servant whose master has gone mad. She
tells him that

this Day fortnight in the Morning a poor simple Child came to him
from the Printer's; the Boy had no sooner enter'd the Room, but he
cry'd out *the Devil was come*. He often stares ghastfully, raves aloud,
and mutters between his Teeth the word *Cator*, or *Cato*, or some such
thing. Now, Doctor, this *Cator* is certainly a *Witch*, and my poor
Master is under an evil Tongue; for I have heard him say *Cator* has
bewitch'd the whole Nation. It pitied my very Heart, to think that
a Man of my Master's Understanding and great Scholarship, who, as
the Child told me, had a book of his own in Print, should talk so out-
ragiously. Upon this I went and laid out a Groat for a Horse-shoe,
which is at this time nail'd on the Threshold of his Door; but I don't
find my Master is at all the better for it; he perpetually starts and runs
to the Window when any one knocks, crying out, *S'death! a Messenger
from the French King! I shall die in the* Bastile.

The Doctor thereupon accompanies the old woman to Dennis's

lodgings, where he finds the ailing writer attended by a "Grammarian." Among the papers littering the rooms are sheets of *Cato*, heavily annotated. Poor Dennis is quite out of his head:

DR. He raves, he raves; Mr. *Lintott*, I pray you pinion down his Arms, that he may do no Mischief.

DENN. O I am sick, sick to Death!

DR. That is a good Symptom, a very good Symptom. To be sick to Death (say the modern Physicians) is an excellent Symptom. When a patient is sensible of his Pain, 'tis half a Cure. Pray, Sir, of what are you sick?

DENN. Of every thing, of every thing. I am sick of the *Sentiments*, of the *Diction*, of the *Protasis*, of the *Epitasis*, and the *Catastrophe*—Alas, what is become of the *Drama*, the *Drama*?

OLD WOM. The *Dram*, Sir? Mr. *Lintott* drank up all the Geneva just now; but I'll go fetch more presently!

DENN. O shameful Want, scandalous Omission! By all Immortals, here is no *Peripoetia*, no Change of Fortune in the Tragedy; Z—— no Change at all.

OLD WOM. Pray, good Sir, be not angry, I'll fetch Change.

During his outburst he accuses Lintot of not publicizing his book efficiently, and he describes Addison's tragedy as "execrable" and "abominable." When help is offered him, he cries out:

Caitiffs stand off; unhand me, Miscreants! Is the Man whose whole Endeavors are to bring the Town to Reason mad? Is the Man who settles Poetry on the Basis of Antiquity mad? Dares any one assert there is a *Peripoetia* in that vile Piece that's foisted upon the Town for a Dramatick Poem? that Man is Mad, the Town is mad, the World is mad. See *Longinus* in my right hand, and *Aristotle* in my left: I am the only Man among the Moderns that support [*sic*] them. Am I to be assassinated? and shall a Bookseller, who hath liv'd upon my Labours, take away that Life to which he owes his Support? [32]

After he has flung everything in sight, including a peruke, at his would-be comforters, they retreat to dress their wounds. At the close he is still mad, and nothing can be done for him.

The value of this *jeu d'esprit*, whether Pope's own or merely a reflection of his attitudes, is that it heaps more fuel on the anti-*Cato* fire. While the sarcasm is directed at Dennis, and exposes the extremes of his temperament, it simultaneously repeats his charges against the play, thus keeping them before the public eye in parody.

In 1714 Pope, probably in collaboration with Rowe, dispatched another little barb at *Cato*. This was a ribald short poem originally called "Upon a Tory Lady who shed her Water at Cato" and given an even more explicit title in the 1727 volume of the Pope-Swift *Miscellanies*. The squib merits quoting here, if only because it has been printed so infrequently:

> While maudlin Whigs deplor'd their *Cato*'s Fate,
> Still with dry Eyes the Tory *Celia* sate,
> But while her Pride forbids her Tears to flow,
> The gushing Waters find a Vent below:
> Tho' secret, yet with copious Grief she mourns,
> Like twenty River-Gods with all their Urns.
> Let others screw their Hypocritick Face,
> She shows her Grief in a sincerer Place;
> There Nature reigns, and Passion void of Art,
> For that Road leads directly to the Heart.[33]

Now that Pope had entered the Tory camp, the Whigs were "maudlin." His emotions about the play had shifted in the course of a year from casual fault-finding, as later reported to Spence, to enthusiasm, as in the first letter to Caryll, to boredom mingled with distaste, as in the poem to Caryll and *The Narrative of Dr. Robert Norris*, to, ultimately, disdain.

Rowe is associated with still another of Pope's hits at *Cato*. To oblige his friend, Pope wrote an Epilogue intended for Rowe's *Tragedy of Jane Shore*, first produced at Drury Lane on February 2, 1714. Oddly enough, the poem was neither spoken on the opening night nor printed with the play and was not published until 1717, when it appeared in Pope's collected works. Perhaps, as one modern scholar believes, Mrs. Oldfield, for whom the poem was intended, refused to speak Pope's lines.[34] Since a discussion of Pope's relations with actors is reserved for a later chapter, it is enough for the moment to consider other matters pertaining to the Epilogue.

The poem is so typical of its kind that its omission from the opening-night proceedings and printed text of the play cannot be the result of the somewhat indelicate tone Pope gave it. The usual contemporary epilogue for tragedy was intended to bring about a complete change of mood from that of the play itself. By custom the speaker jokingly reviewed the tragic situation and went on to decry it. If the play concerned a zealously virtuous woman, she was denounced as silly for refusing a handsome lover. If a woman doubted her husband, she was taunted for lacking the allure to keep him at home. Such epilogues were in dubious taste, to be sure, but the convention was too well established to be abandoned easily. The intention of such pieces was to win applause by setting the audience in a pleasant frame of mind, and Pope's in its manner and style was no different from others of its day.

As another gibe at Addison's play, the piece is amusing, for it is not difficult to imagine how Addison would have reacted to the following lines:

> Well, if our author in the Wife offends,
> He has a Husband that will make amends.
> He draws him gentle, tender, and forgiving,
> And sure such good kind creatures may be living.
> In days of old they pardon'd breach of vows,
> Stern *Cato*'s self was no relentless spouse:
> *Plu—Plutarch,* what's his name that writes his life?
> Tells us, that *Cato* dearly lov'd his wife:
> Yet if a friend a night, or so, should need her,
> He'd recommend her, as a special breeder.
> To lend a wife, few here would scruple make;
> But pray which of you all would take her back?
> Tho' with the Stoick chief our stage may ring,
> The Stoick husband was the glorious thing.
> The man had courage, was a sage, 'tis true,
> And lov'd his country—but what's that to you?
> Those strange examples ne'er were made to fit ye,
> But the kind cuckold might instruct the City:
> There, many an honest man may copy *Cato*,
> Who ne'er saw naked Sword, or look'd in *Plato*.[35]

(ll. 25–44)

It was scarcely in such a mood as this that Addison had designed his hero.

The gradual change in Pope's views on the play may have been brought about by his association with the Scriblerus Club, the informal literary society which counted among its members Swift, Parnell, Arbuthnot, and Gay. Although the club was not established as a political organization, and was, in fact, first suggested by the nonpolitical Pope, its Tory membership soon impressed it with a partisan stamp. While it is true that Pope never abandoned all his Whig friends, such as Rowe and John Hughes, the Scriblerians became his favorite associates. It was inevitable that the strong personality of Swift should affect his political thinking.

For some time before the club was founded, Pope had been considering the possibility of a monthly satire on Grub Street writers. He met Swift in April or May of 1713, possibly through Parnell, and by October he was ready to present the Dean with the plan of a publication of "The Works of the Unlearned." A club was projected to produce the "Works," but not until Christmas, after the recovery of Queen Anne from an alarming illness, were the plans completed. The members then decided to join in writing a series of satires to appear under the authorship of "Martinus Scriblerus," whose name was to stand for dullness and narrow pedantry. Within two years the literary transactions of this society were to draw Pope once more into the theatre, and there to present him with a number of less than pleasant social and literary relationships.[36]

Although the Scriblerians were unable to maintain their club for long, their joint literary activity continued through many years. The group began the writing of the *Memoirs of Martinus Scriblerus*, its best-known collaborative effort, in 1714 at the earliest meetings and took it up again in 1716–18 (in Swift's absence) and in 1726–27. During and after the period indicated by those dates other writings emerged as offshoots of the society. Among these are three unquestioned masterpieces, *Gulliver's Travels*, *The Beggar's Opera*, and the *Dunciad*, as well as two farces, *The What D'ye Call It* and *Three Hours after Marriage*. Each of these works, with the exception of *The Beggar's Opera*, contains subject matter and ideas discussed by the club as a whole. But while *Gulliver*, *The Beg-*

gar's Opera, and the *Dunciad* are respectively the productions of Swift, Gay, and Pope alone, the two farces, though published under Gay's name alone, may have been the result of collaborative effort.

Almost as soon as *The What D'ye Call It* received its successful first performance (at Drury Lane, February 23, 1715), a rumor began to circulate that Gay had found a collaborator in Pope. Those who spread the report seemed to think that to identify Pope with the farce was to damage his reputation. Why this should be so is quite unexplainable, since the play is harmless. But the breach between Pope and Addison was widening, as revealed by the two epigrams on *Cato* and Addison's double dealing over a translation of Homer to rival one of Pope's making, and the frequenters of Button's sensed that Pope was somehow behind the play.[37] No doubt their convictions were supported by its content, which with mock seriousness parodies some of the most enthusiastically praised tragedies of dramatic history, including the inevitable *Cato*.

It was not Gay's purpose, however, to direct the play at *Cato*, or at any other particular work. Labeling the piece "tragi-comi-pastoral farce," he took pains in the introduction to the printed version to justify this mélange. With a list of the objections the critics had raised to the inclusion of the play in any of the specified dramatic categories, he refuted each of their cavils in turn. His particular targets were, obviously, the supporters of the rules, especially those diehards who believed modern plays should contain no devices which the classical dramatists omitted. Gay's Preface, which is an obvious spoof of the contemporary dramatic critics, strikes at such narrow-mindedness by asserting that categories are meaningless, since no emotion can be made to fit a pattern. In his summation Gay clinches the point by sensibly remarking that the premises of the critics must surely be fallacious, because his lawless play was a success.[38]

As a farce, the play succeeds admirably, obtaining most of its humor from parody and from absurd, anticlimactic speeches purposely unsuited to the mock-heroic action. The action itself is constantly ironic, as it must be to obtain full value from the many allusions to other plays. In a play-within-the-play Filbert, a rustic youth, is pressed into military service, to the despair of Kitty, his sweetheart. The plot is complicated by the allegation that another girl has conceived a child by Filbert. These and all other tribulations of the rustics are presented with preposterously high seriousness. As an example of the treatment of past and current dramatic technique, the anxious speech of Kitty over Filbert's long absence will serve. Here the rant of Otway is the model:

> Hah!—I am turn'd a stream—look all below;
> It flows, and flows, and will forever flow.
> The meads are all afloat—the haycocks swim.
> Hah! who comes here!—my *Filbert*! drown not him.
> Bagpipes in butter, flocks in fleecy fountains,
> Churns, sheep-hooks, seas of milk, and honey mountains.[39]

That Gay's technique was effective and that the play was a success are two demonstrable facts. The farce enjoyed twenty-two performances during its first season and was frequently revived during the century. As to the parody of pathos, Pope wrote glowingly to Caryll on March 3:

The farce has occasioned many different speculations in the town, some looked upon it as a mere jest upon the tragic poets, others as a satire upon the late war. Mr. Cromwell hearing none of the words and seeing the action to be tragical, was much astonished to see the audience laugh; and says the Prince and Princess must doubtless be under no less amazement on the same account. Several Templars and others of the more vociferous kind of critics, went with a resolution to hiss, and confessed they were forced to laugh so much that they forgot the design they came with. The Court in general has in a very particular manner come into the jest, and the three first nights (notwithstanding two of them were Court nights) were distinguished by very full audiences of the first quality. The common people of the pit and gallery received it at first with great gravity and sedateness, some few with tears; but after the third day they also took the hint, and have ever since been loud in their clapps. There are still some grave sober men who cannot be of the general opinion, but the laughers are so much the majority, that Mr Dennis and one or two more seem determined to undeceive the town at their proper cost, by writing some critical dissertations against it: to encourage them in which laudable design, it is resolved that a preface shall be prefixt to the farce in the vindication of the nature and dignity of this new way of writing.[40]

Although Pope's letter makes no comment on the collaboration as such, one of the "critical dissertations" at which he hinted insisted that he took part in the writing. This was a pamphlet called *A Complete Key to the last New Farce The What D'ye Call It*, which appeared about two weeks after the publication of the play.[41] On no valid evidence Pope claimed that Benjamin Griffin and Lewis Theobald wrote the piece.[42] Whoever may have written it, the author or authors were convinced that Pope had a hand in it. Without naming him, they declared that

we could expect nothing less from the baseness of a busy Pen, which is now attacking all the Reputations that rais'd its own, and skreens itself behind a borrow'd Name . . . But this *malevolent Critick* fights, like little Teucer, behind a shield of impenetrable stupidity.

. . . .

Where the Maggot first grew, or to what refin'd Head it owes its Original, is kept, as it ought to be, a great Secret. But it must needs have been a merry Scene, to see a Wit and Witling in deep Meditation, to fix the Name of this labourious Performance. How incontinently did they laugh at the Thought of the *Distress'd Damsel*! But then how were they transported at the what d'ye call it! O dear, remote, dull hint at Something![43]

The authors of the pamphlet point out parodies of Shakespeare, Dryden, Southerne, Otway, Lee, Rowe, and Steele, among others, and they emphasize certain humiliations of the lines of Philips and Addison. One instance in particular ruffled them. In *The What D'ye Call It* a miscreant named Peascod just before his death is moved to tears by the title page of *The Pilgrim's Progress*:

Lend me thy handkercher—*The Pilgrim's Pro*—

[*Reads and weeps.*

(I cannot see for tears) *Pro-Progress-*Oh!
*The Pilgrim's Progress—eighth—edi-ti-on
Lon-don-prin-ted—for—Ni-cho-las Bod-ding-ton
With new ad-di-tions never made before.*
Oh! 'tis so moving, I can read no more.

[*Drops the book.*[44]

The authors considered this an especially disrespectful slur at *Cato*, for Addison's hero had read Plato before his death, and *Cato*, like the copy of *The Pilgrim's Progress* which Peascod reads, had just gone into an eighth edition![45]

To what extent is the charge justified that Pope helped to write the play? Others than the authors of the *Complete Key* have insisted that he did. Dennis twice pressed the point, first in his *Remarks on Pope's Homer* in 1717 and, as late as 1728, in a rebuttal to the *Peri Bathous*.[46] Another enemy, Colley Cibber, related to Spence, perhaps with exaggeration, that "Mr. Pope brought some of the 'What d'ye call it,' in his own hand writing to Cibber, the part about the miscarriage in particular, but not much beside. When it was read to the players, Mr. Pope read it, though Gay was by.—Gay always used to read his own plays. After this upon seeing a knife with the name of J. Gay upon it, Cibber said; 'What, does Mr. Pope make knives too?' "[47]

Pope's participation, then, has been frequently asserted. There is certainly good ground to believe him at least a contributor, if not a full collaborator, for in 1715 Pope was collecting those banal lines from the drama which ultimately appeared in the *Peri Bathous* and which, generally, are akin to the lines made fun of in *The What D'ye Call It*.[48] Moreover, as has been sufficiently demonstrated, Pope had already given a considerable amount of thought to *Cato*. The cooperative system of the Scriblerus Club is another factor, for during the writing of the *Memoirs* Pope and Gay had already learned to work together. And, though it is scarcely final proof, the play exhibits the same tongue-in-cheek earnestness underlying the ribald epigrams on *Cato*.

Somewhat more difficult to accept is a recent theory that Pope and Gay wrote the *Key*.[49] The pamphlet is too serious in tone, and too bitter in its condemnation of Pope to be intended as a joke. Charles Kerby-Miller argues unconvincingly that the two weeks between the publication of the play and the pamphlet would not have allowed enough time for anyone unfamiliar with the play to prepare the *Key*. To a person interested in the literature of the theatre a few days would have been sufficient.

The What D'ye Call It served as a trial performance for the writing of still another farce, *Three Hours after Marriage*, which began its career at Drury Lane on January 16, 1717. Arbuthnot, who had not worked on the earlier play, joined with Pope and Gay in preparing the new one. Pope's contribution was at least the Prologue and probably much more, although Gay alone acknowledged the piece. Probably no secret activity of Pope's career was more poorly guarded than his work on this play. Despite the obvious fact that *Three Hours* was not intended to be a party piece, rumors concerning it were reaching Whig circles several days before the first performance.[50] Yet those who expected to find pointed partisan material were disappointed (though nonetheless abusive), for *Three Hours*, in the Scriblerian manner, boisterously lampoons false learning rather than faulty political philosophy. In it Dr. Woodward, a well-known if not altogether reliable physician and "virtuoso," received the brunt of the onslaught, while a good share was directed at Dennis and Colley Cibber.

Because of its bawdiness *Three Hours* has not received the recognition it deserves. Like all farces, the play gets its humor from repetition, exaggeration, and quaint logic. If it makes use of stock types, it has the virtue, at least, of revitalizing them with certain characteristics of specific persons. The plot, in brief, recounts the commonplace tale of an old, suspicious husband's troubles with a newly acquired wife. In the play the husband, Dr. Fossile, is given every reason to be suspicious, for his wife, Townley, begins to carry on an affair as soon as the wedding ceremony is accomplished. Plotwell, an actor-manager, is the object of Townley's interest, and he contrives a number of farcical devices in order to be alone with her, even going so far as to play on Fossile's love of science by draping himself as a mummy while Underplot, his shadow, appears disguised as a crocodile. The intrigue is advanced through the activity of Phoebe Clinket, Fossile's playwright niece, who has asked Plotwell to look at her latest manuscript. Townley and Plotwell read the parts, interpolating their own private words into them. Through this piece of plotting the authors have the opportunity to present Sir Tremendous Longinus, a great critic, who reads the play and renders it suitable for staging by literally tearing out parts of it. Ultimately Townley is exposed, but only after her deception of Fossile is complete. When three hours have elapsed, the marriage is not only unconsummated but ended.

The authors freshened this admittedly old material with much tomfoolery. Dr. Fossile is not just an aged cuckold, he is also a fool whose scholarly proclivities prevent his being rational. As a collector of scientific specimens and rarities, he thinks of his wife as another item for his shelves and cases. When she feigns bridal fears, the words with which he chooses to soothe her are, "Courage, thou best of my Curiosities." His infatuation with medicine is used to excellent advantage later in the play, when he prescribes treatment for Underplot, who pretends to be overcome by illness in order to gain entrance to the house:

All this proceeds from the Fumes of the Kitchen, the Stomachick Digester wants reparation for the better Concoction of your Ailment: But, Sir, is your Pain pungitive, tensive, gravitive or pulsatory?

. . . .

Your doler proceeds from a Frigid *intemperies* of the Brain, a strong Disease! the Enemy has invaded the very Citadel of your Microcosm, the Magazine of your vital Functions; he has sate down before it; yet there seems to be a good Garrison of vital Spirits, and we don't question to be able to defend it.

. . . .

True, we might unload the Stomach by gentle Emeticks, and the Intestines by Clysters stimulative, carminative, and emollient, with strong Hydropticks, quiet the spasms of the Viscera by Paregoricks, draw off the stagnant Blood by deep Scarrifications, and depurate its Faeculencies by Volatiles; after this, let there be numerous Blisters and potential Cauteries—I consult my Patient's case; I am against much Physick—he faints, he is Apoplectick, bleed him this Moment.[51]

A considerable share of the comedy lies in the characterizations of Plotwell and Sir Tremendous, for whom Cibber and Dennis, respectively, were the models. Pomposity and egoism such as Plotwell's are always amusing when set within the framework of a farce. Much of the humor of the part is left to the actor. Cibber played it, and it was designed for him. The authors, being familiar with his skill in playing fops, wrote

economically. But the treatment of Sir Tremendous is different, for here the humor arises from the man's intemperance:

> SIR TREM. Alas! what signifies one good Palate when the Taste
> of the whole Town is violated. There is not in all this *Sodom* of
> ignorance Ten righteous Criticks, who do not judge things backward.
>
> CLINK. I perfectly agree with Sir *Tremendous*: Your modern
> Tragedies are such egregious Stuff, they neither move Terror nor Pity.
>
> PLOTW. Yes, Madam, the pity of the Audience on the First Night,
> and the Terror of the Author for the Third. Sir *Tremendous*'s Plays
> have rais'd a sublimer Passion, Astonishment.[52]

In a careful study of the events surrounding the presentation
of *Three Hours*, George Sherburn has shown that it was a mod-
est success. It was given seven consecutive performances at
Drury Lane, one more than any other play at that theatre during the season. However, the advantages of a fair run did not
include protection for the play or its authors from abuse. In an
Advertisement prefacing the printed version, Gay had confessed,
"I must further own the Assistance I have receiv'd in this Piece
from two of my Friends; who, tho' they will not allow me the
Honour of having their Names join'd with mine, cannot deprive
me of the Pleasure of making this Acknowledgement." These
two friends were known to be Pope and Arbuthnot. Despite
their wished-for anonymity, they soon became the victims of
severe attacks.

Among the earliest carping commentaries was a *Complete
Key* to the farce prepared by E. Parker two weeks after the
first performance.[53] It was Parker's purpose to identify the
personages who served as models for the characters in the play,
and, accordingly, he identified Plotwell as Cibber, Fossile as
Woodward, Phoebe Clinket as the Countess of Winchilsea, and
Townley as Mrs. Mead, the wife of Pope's physician.[54] Of
course, some of these were obvious from the content of the
play itself, but others were probably no more than quick guesses.
While the parts played by Cibber and Woodward were unquestionable, Parker may have been quite wrong about the two
ladies. Sherburn has argued that Townley is only a stock type
who bears no resemblance to Mrs. Mead, and that Phoebe
Clinket is actually Susanna Centlivre.[55] However, the claim
that Clinket represents Mrs. Centlivre is in turn open to ques-

tion. The principal slur on Clinket, that she has difficulty in achieving productions of her plays, does not easily apply to Mrs. Centlivre, who saw her works performed year after year. On the other hand, Pope had lampooned her the previous year in his series of pieces on the pirate-publisher Edmund Curll.[56] She must have seen some references to herself in *Three Hours*, for she joined the large group of writers who continued the attack on the play long after it had been retired from the Drury Lane repertory.[57]

Sir Tremendous Longinus, easily identified as John Dennis, needs no commentary. Pope had quarreled with him at length, and Gay addressed him very ironically in the Dedication to *The Mohocks* in 1712. More than anything else, the name itself gives him away, for "tremendous" was a part of his critical vocabulary, and he had been one of the earliest champions of Longinus's *Sublime*.

Cibber's appearance as Plotwell presents an interesting question. Was he aware when Gay brought him the play that in Plotwell he would be acting a satire on himself? Sherburn conjectures that Cibber caught on slowly to the authors' prank, not recognizing himself in the role at the start.[58] This is debatable, however, for Cibber was far too shrewd to be duped by such a scheme. From the early years of his career, after he had invented the perfect part for himself as Sir Novelty Fashion in *Love's Last Shift* and had gone on in an extension of the role in Vanbrugh's *The Relapse*, he had shown complete awareness of his own abilities and limitations. Moreover, if at this distance in time the source of Plotwell is obvious, it must have been immediately recognizable in 1717. Rather than be made a fool of by some other actor, Cibber quite likely realized the potential humor of the situation and went ahead with the play. The satire, for that matter, is not so very objectionable—if one possesses a sense of humor.

In an attempt to malign the collaborators Parker also mentioned some curious backstage activity during the performances of *Three Hours*. This was taken up and supplemented in a pamphlet titled *The Confederates*, published on March 30,[59] more than two months after the first performance of the play. *The Confederates* was the work of Capt. John Durant Breval, a member of Curll's stable of writers and an army officer with important Whig connections. Disguising himself under the pseudonym of "Joseph Gay," he fashioned a rhyming farce out of all the gossip to which *Three Hours* gave rise. The title page of the published play bears an engraving of the trio of authors, the tiny Pope between Arbuthnot in highland dress and Gay with cap and bells. In his Introduction Breval, capitalizing on his alias, protests to the reader, *"but the World, I hope, is too Generous to condemn a whole family, because one of its Branches falls under its Censure . . ."*[60] Continuing, he makes it clear that he intends to expose Pope and Arbuthnot, even though his "kinsman" would not.

Although it is obvious from the beginning of *The Confederates* that Breval intends to damage all three writers, the reader soon discovers that Pope is to receive the greatest share of abuse. The Prologue, especially vile, brings to mind Dennis's *The True Character of Mr. Pope*, published the previous year:

> *No far-fetched* Mummies *on this* Stage *appear*,
> *Nor* Snake, *nor* Shark, *nor* Crocodile *is here*;
> *But*, One Strange Monster *we design to show*,
> (*His* Fellow *you ne'er saw* in Channel-Row)
> *On whom Dame Nature nothing good bestow'd*,
> *In* Form, *a* Monkey; *but for* Spite, *a* Toad.
> *Nor thought we fit*, (*since* They *might take it ill*)
> *To leave here his* Brethren of the Quill;
> *The* Northern Doctor *with his* Highland Face;
> *Nor t'other* Wit *that waited on her* Grace.[61]

Breval then proceeds to unfold a most intriguing tale.

The Confederates dramatizes certain alleged machinations of the three authors during and immediately following the first performance of their farce. Pope himself opens the piece, in soliloquy, boasting of his venomous satires. He, not Gay, will get the credit for the play's success, but Gay will take all the risks. At this point in Pope's monologue, Arbuthnot enters, overhears, and is displeased by Pope's claim to have invented all the characters except Fossile. The two men have a quarrel in which Pope uses sharp language on his friend: "Not BUT-TON's Wits from my Lampoons are free, / And Thou, and

BLACKMORE are but *Worms* to me."[62] Pope, however, is easily cowed by the larger man, and, mumbling that he mistook Arbuthnot for Gay, he asks forgiveness. Obviously, Breval hoped to create the impression that Pope was habitually deceitful. The tension is broken when Gay announces that the play has been hissed and the authors must seek the means to save their work from disaster. One suggestion is that they pack the house with thieves, beggars, and schoolboys.

The remainder of the sketch reveals the efforts of the three men to keep their farce on the boards. Everyone has turned against them—the actresses Oldfield and Bicknell, Cibber, and even the publisher Bernard Lintot. The first blow is struck by the leading ladies, who will not work unless granted a generous bonus. Mrs. Oldfield is primarily to blame, for she is determined to drop her role at once, having been thoroughly offended by the noises from the audience. Mrs. Bicknell, to find a way out, suggests the gift. Gay, making a counteroffer, proposes, "If you have Male or Female Foes, / These Sawney shall lampoon, I'll challenge Those."[63] But this will not do; only money will keep the actresses in the play. It is possible that this part of Breval's plot may be based on truth, since Pope was no admirer of Mrs. Oldfield, as his spreading—if not actually writing—the epigram on "Cato's daughter" demonstrated. On the other hand, proof exists that Mrs. Bicknell was on the best of terms with Pope before and after *Three Hours*, since he wrote pleasantly of her in "A Farewell to London. In the Year 1715," and Gay included her in the group welcoming Pope on his "return from Greece" (the completion of his laborious translation of Homer) in 1720. If the actresses did make an attempt at extortion, it is quite likely that Mrs. Bicknell was less to blame than her illustrious colleague.

More fascinating is the hint that Pope promised aid to Cibber in his adaptation of Corneille's *Le Cid* in return for Cibber's keeping the play on. Cibber, annoyed at being jeered as a mummy, refuses ever to put the costume on again. Pope, to conciliate him, says, "Come let thy Talent lye no longer hid, / I'll to Perfection bring thy mighty *Cid* . . ." But, once the bargain is made, he adds in soliloquy that he will never do it:

"By G——, I'll serve him as I serv'd the rest."⁶⁴ The argument
is made also by Parker in the *Complete Key* that Cibber "has
also Naturaliz'd the *Cid* of *Corneille* into an *English Heroick
Daughter*, Which will see the Light, as soon as Mr. *Pope* has
touch'd it up, who has it now for that Purpose, the Diction
being somewhat *obnubilated*."⁶⁵ That both pamphleteers should
make this point compels attention. *Ximena: or, The Heroick
Daughter*, Cibber's adaptation, first appeared at Drury Lane
in 1712, was revived in 1718, and was published in octavo in
1719. Was *Ximena* as produced in 1718 a revised play?
The printed text nowhere gives evidence of Pope's hand. The
possibility that Pope did break his promise to Cibber, as Breval
had it, is greater than that he came to Cibber's aid, for the playwright's Preface seems (but only seems) to strike at him. Of
persons who damn plays, Cibber writes:

But I have seen frequent Instances, that the same sort of Auditors,
with a little Management, have been made as enterprizing Friends
to other Authors, as they were then Enemies to me: For with some
leading Man of the Town, or celebrated Wit at the Head of them,
they have been often known, by their over bearing Manner of Applause, to make a wretched sickly Play stand stoutly upon its Legs
for Six Days together . . . And if in Breach of [my] Resolution
[not to write more plays], I have since attempted in the *Non-juror*
to expose the enemies of our Constitution, and Liberties, it was because
I knew the Friends of the Government would secure me a fair hearing, and from all such Apprehensions of being disturbed by the wanton
Malice of a few Petits Maitres.⁶⁶

If it is true that some pump-priming was necessary to keep
Three Hours going, Cibber may have been remembering the
occasion.

Ultimately, in Breval's version of the *Three Hours* affair,
the situation is saved by a gift from G[riffi]n, B[ellende]ne,
and L[ep]p[el]l, who send money and a note of admiration.
These are the three court ladies whom Pope addressed with
much cordiality the same year in "The Challenge." He was
to write twenty-one years later, moreover, that Timon, "if
three Ladies like a luckless Play, / Takes the whole House upon
the Poet's Day"⁶⁷—possibly an allusion to the same three ladies.

This fascinating pamphlet, then, seems based in part on fact. Everything in it (except, it would be pleasant to think, the scene between Pope and Arbuthnot) could have occurred. How are we to account for such familiarity with Pope's private life as Breval disclosed? It may have been, of course, that Curll, Breval's sometime employer, gave him information, whether genuine or fabricated. But a stronger possibility is that Whig forces engineered an attempt to blacken the three writers. Pope at least suspected that party matters were behind some of the abuse, because he wrote to Parnell of the rising "tide of malice and party" against the play, and later told Spence that Addison and his friends objected to it because of its obscenity.[68] Yet, Pope, who came off worse in the attacks than either of his friends, was not so strongly partisan as to deserve harsh treatment.

In the postlude to *Three Hours* Cibber again appeared as principal actor. Whether because he resented acting himself in the character of Plotwell, because he sensed that Pope would go back on a bargain to revise his tragedy, or—the most likely reason—because he knew a good thing in the theatre when he saw it, Cibber soon made up for his disappointment with the three collaborators by burlesquing one of their scenes. On February 7 Cibber revived *The Rehearsal*, and, following the established custom of including in Buckingham's play any new business which could be expected to draw laughter, he satirized the piece of foolery from *Three Hours* involving the mummy and crocodile. According to a much later account of the revival which Cibber himself wrote, Pope, hopping mad at this insult to his literary genius, dashed backstage to threaten Cibber with violence. Cibber, calm and capable, put off the sputtering playwright with a few carefully chosen words.[69] Cibber may or may not have been inventing the tale, but the picture of the little Pope, choking with inarticulate fury, confronted by the self-collected actor, is as amusing as any scene in the play he was so quick to defend.

Although *Three Hours after Marriage* was not revived for twenty years, and then at Lincoln's Inn Fields rather than at Drury Lane, it was not soon forgotten. One prologue and sev-

eral pantomimes kept its memory fresh at least for a while.
The Prologue to Charles Johnson's *The Sultaness* struck a re-
taliating blow within a month. Whereas Pope in his Prologue
to *Three Hours* had deplored, as always, the fact that too many
adaptations were cluttering the London stage, the anonymous
author of Johnson's Prologue defended them:

> *Our honest Author frankly bid me say,*
> *'Tis to the Great* Racine *he owes his Play:*
>
> .   .   .   .
>
> *At least, 'tis hoped, he'll meet a kinder Fate*
> *Who strives some* Standard *Author to translate,*
> *Than they, who give you, without once repenting,*
> *Long-labour'd Nonsense of their own inventing.*
> *Such Wags have been, who boldly durst adventure*
> *To Club a Farce by Tripartite-Indenture:*
> *But, let them share a Dividend of Praise,*
> *And their own* Fools-Cap *wear, instead of Bays.*[70]

The pantomimes seem to have been attempts to work over
the antics of the mummy and crocodile. Two of them, *The
Shipwreck; or, Perseus and Andromeda* and *The Jealous Doctor; or, The Intriguing Dame,* which were never published,
were staged in April. A third, Mrs. Aubert's *Harlequin-
Hydaspes: or, The Greshamite,* which was produced in May
1719, is primarily a satire on Dr. Woodward, but it effectively
parodies a bit of clowning in *Three Hours* in which Fossile is
frustrated by an impertinent apothecary while attempting to
prescribe a remedy.

This discussion of *Three Hours* has given no indication of
the extent of Pope's share in the play. Gay's Advertisement
merely acknowledges assistance but does not give the poet's
name. Breval's testimony that Pope invented all the characters
except Fossile is questionable, since Gay, as a professional playwright, could be expected to carry the heaviest part of the work.
At this late date the task of assigning lines to each of the three
writers would be impossible. It should be noted, nevertheless,
that the tone of the play was not outside the scope of Pope's
talents. The Curll pamphlets and *The Rape of the Lock,*

which preceded the play, have as much or perhaps even more of the same wit, satire, and high spirit.

Pope's theatrical writing after this was somewhat tamer in its effect on the public and his critics. Never again willing to compose dramatic dialogue, he occasionally took up his pen to serve his theatrical friends in other ways. Among the first of these friends was John Sheffield, sixth Duke of Buckingham, a poetaster and patron of writers of greater talent than his own. Sheffield had divided Shakespeare's *Julius Caesar* into two parts, one consisting of the events surrounding Caesar's assassination and the other of Brutus's subsequent career. Both were neo-classical tragedies of the most "regular" variety. Appearing in the 1717 edition of Pope's *Works,* but possibly published earlier, were two choruses to be sung after the first and second acts of *Brutus*. Although never acted, the play and the choruses were set to music by Buononcini and performed at Buckingham House on January 10, 1723, after the Duke himself had died.[71] At the Duchess of Buckingham's request Pope had written to Lord Percival to ask for his intervention with Colonel Hunter, one of the directors of the Opera, for a performance at Drury Lane. When it was reported that Colonel Hunter was unable to oblige, the performance at Buckingham House was undertaken. The Duchess had expected also that Pope would provide a prologue, but this he was unable to do.[72]

Since Sheffield's plays are analyzed in the next chapter, it is enough to remark here that Pope's choruses, whether acted or sung, are scarcely suitable as dramatic poetry. Sheffield had reduced Shakespeare's verse to "pure" but stilted diction, and Pope followed the style closely. The choruses are so cold and elegant, so uncontrasting to the play proper, that they lack distinction even as ornaments. Very much to the point is a further charge made by Joseph Warton that, by doing nothing to advance the action of *Brutus* and consequently having no organic connection with it, they "might be inserted with equal propriety in twenty other tragedies."[73]

When Gay reached the high point of his fame with *The Beggar's Opera,* it was to be expected that Pope, his most intimate friend, should be regarded as a contributor to the play. Apparently it was taken for granted among literary circles that the earlier collaborative association should continue. Persons hostile to Pope saw an opportunity to damage him by stressing his alignment with anti-Walpole forces. Thus William Broome, piqued that he had been ill rewarded for his labors on Pope's translation of the *Odyssey*, wrote maliciously to Elijah Fenton on May 3, 1728:

I have seen Mr. Gay's mock opera. Johnny is a good-natured inoffensive man. I doubt not, therefore, but those lines against courts and ministers are drawn, at least aggravated, by Mr. Pope, who delights to paint every man in the worst colours. He wounds from behind Gay, and like Teucer in Homer, puts Gay in the front of the battle, and shoots his arrows lurking under the shield of Ajax.[74]

One year after the death of Pope, William Ayre in his complimentary biography attributed to Pope many of "the Squibs [in *The Beggar's Opera*] that were thrown at the Court." Also, according to Ayre, Pope rewrote the last two lines of Peachum's notorious song "Thro' all the Employments of Life" in an attempt to make them sharper, and contributed the entire song "Since Laws are made for ev'ry Degree."[75] Since Pope never admitted making any important additions to the play, these claims cannot be proved or disproved. He told Spence that although Gay wrote his ballad opera in the very house where he and Swift were working, neither of them "did more than alter an expression here and there."[76] They "now and then gave a correction, or a word or two of advice," but that was all.

Ayre continued his commentary with the information that "Mr. *Pope* encouraged Mr. *Gay* to write the Sequel [*Polly*], and to write it still more severe against the Court";[77] but on this point Pope was silent. Nor did he comment on Alexander Burnet's charge that he, Arbuthnot, and Pulteney wrote some of the songs for Gay's posthumous *Achilles*.[78]

These charges, originating with persons hostile to Pope, were obviously contrived to belittle or endanger the poet for his antiadministration sympathies. The truth has not been discovered, but it is unlikely that Pope might have hidden behind Gay, as Broome suggests, for fear of detection. No other writer of the period was less cautious than Pope in concealing his temperament.

Pope's final work in the theatre marked the terminal point of his long quarrel with Dennis. In 1733 Dennis, then seventy-seven years old, received a benefit performance at the New Theatre in the Haymarket of Cibber's *The Provok'd Husband*, and Pope, possibly at the instigation of James Thomson,[79] wrote the Prologue. Although the poem was far from eulogistic, with its reference to Dennis's infirmities and his foolish invention of a thunder machine, it did, as Ruffhead observed, make "a very serious recommendation of him to the audience."[80] Pope's action in befriending the old man was generous, for in 1717 Dennis had written of him in astonishingly harsh language.

With this Prologue the record of Pope's creative activity in the theatre closes. It is not a lengthy record: sessions with Addison and Gay provide the most substantial entries, but even these are more notable for the disputes and complex personal relationships they generated than for service to dramatic art. But the experience gave him useful knowledge of the playwright's craft which he was often to draw upon for other purposes in the next two decades.

II

CONSULTANT TO PLAYWRIGHTS
(1720's)

ALTHOUGH the petty annoyances of *Three Hours after Marriage* may have seemed interminable, they did not demolish Pope's regard for the stage. In the decades of the 1720's and 1730's it was his constant practice to read the manuscripts of would-be playwrights who hoped to gain his support. The plays of the 1720's were useful in the development of Pope's taste in the drama and the crystallization of most of his critical principles. In the period of the second decade, which is to be discussed in the next chapter, Pope applied his knowledge to, among other plays, a group of political tragedies.

In both periods the manuscripts were accompanied by requests of four kinds: for an opinion, for a prologue or an epilogue, for advice on revisions, or for intervention with the managers. Except when asked for prologues or epilogues, Pope was astonishingly generous. Nowhere in his correspondence appears a refusal to read a play. As the evidence reveals, after 1719 Pope commented on or worked over fifteen new manuscripts and at least one refurbished play.[1]

Activity of this kind was not new to Pope, for he had begun as early as 1713 with *Cato* to provide dramatists with editorial assistance. On December 15 of that year he wrote to John Caryll that he had attended a play-reading at the home of the Countess of Winchilsea, despite a disagreeable illness.[2] (Unfortunately, he failed to pass along the name of the play or its author.) From the time of this incident to 1720 he seems to have been too busy with other matters (including the two farces in collaboration with Gay) to look at other manuscripts, but by 1734 he had read enough of them to complain eloquently in the *Epistle to Dr. Arbuthnot*:

> Bless me! a Packet.—" 'Tis a stranger sues,
> "A Virgin Tragedy, an Orphan Muse."
> If I dislike it, "Furies, death and rage!"
> If I approve, "Commend it to the Stage."
> There (thank my Stars) my whole Commission ends,
> The Play'rs and I are, luckily, no friends.
> Fir'd that the House reject him, " 'Sdeath I'll print it
> "And shame the Fools—your Int'rest, Sir, with *Lintot*."
> *Lintot*, dull rogue! will think your price too much.
> "Not Sir, if you revise it, and retouch."
> All my demurrs but double his attacks,
> At last he whispers "Do and we go snacks."
> Glad of a quarrel, strait I clap the door,
> Sir, let me see your works and you no more.[3]

(ll. 55–68)

But despite this protest he gave aid whenever he was asked for it.

Why did Pope read and revise these plays? First, his strong curiosity about all aspects of theatrical art probably led him to read most of the manuscripts, although it is certainly difficult to imagine what amount of pleasure they gave him. Pope had, after all, taken his part with obvious spirit in preparing *Cato* and *Three Hours* for the stage. Moreover, he had exhibited acute concern throughout Gay's career in the theatre. Another equally valid reason was his innate benevolence, even to strangers if they had not offended him. Thus he looked at plays by such little-known men as David Lewis, Thomas Whincop, and an obscure footman, Robert Dodsley, who was later to become his publisher. Obligation and friendship led him to read Elijah Fenton's tragedy, and for personal as well as political reasons he assisted James Thomson, Aaron Hill, and David Mallet. His own widely publicized early work in the theatre and his edition of Shakespeare, which was begun in the early 1720's, were reflections of his interest, and aspiring playwrights may have been encouraged by them to send him their manuscripts.

It is noteworthy that all but two of the new plays submitted to Pope were tragedies and that of the two exceptions, one was a "dramatic satire" and the other a romance. Inasmuch as he was known to have collaborated on *Three Hours* and had been very friendly with Wycherley and Congreve, it may seem curious that no comic writers brought their work to him. Yet the reason for this emphasis on tragedy is not difficult to grasp. Among those men who hoped to enrich the world by means of their literary works, tragedy was the preferred genre. In the Augustan age, as in any other, writers held tragedy to be the most significant dramatic form. Because of the great prestige Pope had won for himself by the 1720's, in the social world as well as in the literary, young writers of comedy were probably less inclined to send him their plays than were writers of tragedy. To have asked the great Mr. Pope to criticize a lighter work would have been to bother him with a trifle. The one exception was Robert Dodsley, who in the mid-1730's asked and received Pope's efforts on behalf of *The Toy-Shop* and *The King and the Miller of Mansfield*. But Dodsley, though a bookman, had no literary pretensions; he seems primarily to have hoped to relieve the poverty which was his lot as a footman. Yet tragedy was never so popular as those who created it wished to believe, and few of the tragedies examined by Pope succeeded with the public.[4]

The chronicle of Pope's career as adviser to playwrights begins in 1720, when he examined John Hughes's *The Siege of Damascus*. As though a portent of the future, no play could have been more precisely representative of the fifteen tragedies placed into his hands during the next two decades. With his kindly treatment of Hughes, one of his cronies in the old days at Button's, Pope set the pattern which he was to follow in attending to the wants of other playwrights: a complimentary letter on first reading the play, a polite but firm refusal to supply a prologue, and a note on his schedule of activities for the opening night.

In mid-January 1720 Hughes petitioned Pope for a prologue and asked, as well, that he read the tragedy. Pope replied that an illness made it impossible for him to supply the verses, but he was careful to give Hughes several pleasant compliments to make up for his refusal.[5] Although there is no reason to suppose that Pope was anything but truthful in the letter, it is worth noting that he was loath to compose prologues and epilogues on any occasion. After 1717 he honored only two requests for them. His reluctance was usually due, as he explained to William Broome, to his awareness that he could not conceal his authorship.[6] He may have remembered too well the first night of *Cato*, when he was "clapped into a staunch Whig" as the result of his Prologue.

He was willing, however, to read through the play. Shortly before it went into performance, he wrote again to Hughes: "I return the play sooner than I am willing to part with what I like so extremely well, because you press it."[7] This message was nothing more than an expression of general approval, but it must have been welcome to Hughes, who, though dangerously ill, was hastily readying his play for the stage.

On February 17, 1720, *The Siege of Damascus* began its successful run at Drury Lane—a run which its author did not live to see. Poor Hughes, in far more tragic plight than his hero, died of consumption on the very night of his only triumph in the theatre. Unaware of this, Pope had written to say that he too was ill and could not attend the first performance.[8] Perhaps Hughes was able to take some comfort in the fact that Pope wished him to secure a side box for some "particular friends," for surely Pope must have admired the play if he intended to send friends to it. With ready sympathy he wrote on February 26 to Jabez Hughes, the playwright's brother, "I believe I am further obliged to you for his Play; which I rec'd yesterday & read over again, with more Concern & Sorrow than I ever felt at reading any Tragedy."[9] Just as the unhappy occasion colored Pope's remark, so it probably contributed to the success of the play—with the assistance of some publicity by Steele in *The Theatre*.[10]

The play, which is typical of the standard fare of the period, has no particular merits of its own. Like *Cato* and the many others which were to come, *The Siege of Damascus* is a well-constructed, "regular," pathetic, and fustian tragedy. It presents a romantic account of the attempts by Christians in Damascus to withstand a prolonged Saracen attack. Phocyas,

the leader of the Christian forces, is so disturbed by the refusal
of his suit for Eudocia, the governor's daughter, that he betrays
Damascus. In time he repents, kills the Saracen leader, and is
himself slain by the enemy. In strict accordance with the requirements of neoclassicism, no subplot interferes with the
principal action. Indeed, the entire tragedy is concentrated on
the play of emotions within Phocyas, who turns from anger
when the governor ignores his suit to despair after he has betrayed his city. The meaning of unity of place is interpreted
to include the city and the territory surrounding it, but the
principle is not seriously violated. Unity of time is treated in
a way which had long since become standard: so much action
is crammed into the five acts that no definite account can be
made of the hours involved, with the result that "time" becomes
"timelessness." But in the indistinct period covered by the
action so many reversals occur that the result is hopeless
monotony. The primary element of tragedy, man's eventual
awareness of the implications of his actions, is not present in
the play. Here the "tragic" hero experiences remorse only
because his beloved denounces his deeds, not because he recog-
nizes the evil in them, and it is only by chance that a Saracen
arrow fells him.

One may well ask how Pope, whose poetry attests to his
acuteness, could profess to enjoy Hughes's play. This was the
second tragedy of its sort to give him pleasure, and it was far
from the last. But it must be remembered that Hughes was his
friend, and one is usually inclined to speak well of a friend's
work. Yet this cannot have been all, for many years later when
Hughes's name came up in conversation with Spence, Pope,
remembering *The Siege of Damascus,* remarked that Hughes
was "but a poor writer, except his play, that is very well."[11] It
is unfortunate that Pope when criticizing tragedy did not always
exercise that exactness of judgment which his contempt for
Grub Street has led modern-day readers to expect from him.
Even in his own century it was remarked that he failed to be
perceptive when appraising drama: a later writer considered
Pope's support of another neoclassical tragedy, Thomson's
Agamemnon, to be evidence of his ineptness in criticism.[12] But

Pope, to whom classical restraint was a virtue, was committed to admire a work molded in a tightly constricting form. The rigidity of the requirements within which a playwright was compelled to work was approved as strongly by Pope as by his lesser contemporaries.

Hughes's play appears almost loose in its construction when compared to the two severely controlled plays by John Sheffield, Duke of Buckingham, which Pope turned to next. Sheffield's two adaptations of Shakespeare, *The Tragedy of Julius Caesar* and *The Tragedy of Marcus Brutus,* had been written earlier in the century, and Pope had designed two choruses for the latter play at some undiscoverable date before printing them in the 1717 edition of his collected poems.[13] After the Duke's death in 1721 Pope became his literary executor, an office which required him to read Sheffield's tragedies and to prepare them for publication. It is not possible to say whether Pope altered the plays while readying them for the press, but the likelihood that he did so is strong, for he could rarely read anything without retouching it. A larger question surrounds his ability to concern himself at all with two such extraordinarily dull works. Friendship is once more the likeliest explanation. As early as the year in which he wrote the *Essay on Criticism*—1709 by Pope's dating—Pope and Sheffield had been friends. Twice in the *Essay* Pope echoes Sheffield's own *Essay on Poetry* and once quotes it directly.[14] To be sure, Pope was not entirely uncritical of Sheffield's work, for he confided to Spence after the Duke's death, "The Duke of Buckingham was superficial in everything; even in poetry, which was his *fort*."[15]

Despite these reservations, it is very likely that Pope admired the Duke's attempt to regularize Shakespeare. Whereas Shakespeare's *Julius Caesar* ignores the unities, each of Sheffield's tragedies taken from it is a model of regularity. Caesar and Brutus have plays to themselves, with no interfering minor actions. Furthermore, Sheffield's division of Shakespeare's *Julius Caesar* into two parts enabled him to observe the unity of place, of which he was very conscious. Caesar's play takes place only in Rome; and while Brutus's must move from Athens to Philippi, Sheffield's Prologue carefully apologizes for the move.[16] Such "improvements" rendered the plays even more severely rigid than the others Pope had examined previously.

Possibly, too, Pope admired Sheffield's poetic style, inasmuch as the diction of his choruses matches it closely. Precise language, hiding any sign of passion under a smooth surface, is the sole quality of the verse which Sheffield and Pope provided for the tragedies. In this connection, there is evidence that Pope so esteemed Sheffield's taste that he based five of his emendations of Shakespeare's *Julius Caesar* on lines in Sheffield's adaptation. From 1721 through 1724 the two writers were much on his mind, and in at least two letters of 1721 and 1722, to Jacob Tonson and John Caryll, he pondered both editions-in-progress.[17] A comparison of Pope's text of Shakespeare with the Duke's play reveals the extent of the Duke's influence.

Two of these emendations correct double superlatives to normal usage. Since Pope retained Shakespeare's double comparatives and superlatives as often as he corrected them, it is likely that he was inspired to reduce Antony's famous "This is the most unkindest cut of all" to "This, this was the unkindest cut of all" on seeing Sheffield's "This, this was the unkindest Stroke of all!"[18] Similarly, Cassius's "with the most boldest, and best hearts in Rome," which is drastically altered in Sheffield's play to "With all the best and boldest Sons of *Rome*," becomes in Pope's text "With the most bold, and the best hearts of *Rome*."[19]

A third, and otherwise inexplicable verbal alteration, of the first-folio reading of Brutus's "Romans, Countrey-men, and Lovers" to "*Romans*, Countrey-men, and Friends," is understandable if inexcusable when compared with Sheffield's "Friends, dearest Countrymen, and worthy *Romans*."[20] Here Pope adopted Sheffield's three appellatives but retained Shakespeare's order.

Of the many passages which Pope "degraded" to the bottom of the page in his edition as probable interpolations, one is omitted entirely by Sheffield in a speech otherwise following Shakespeare conscientiously. Two lines, "Now is it Rome indeed, and roome enough/When there is in it but one onely man," are cut from a speech of Cassius.[21] Since to the modern ear, at least, these have the ring of the lines which precede and follow them, it again would seem that Pope suspended his judgment to follow Sheffield.

The final example is Pope's assignment to Casca of five and a half lines, beginning "Stoop, Romans, stoop," which in the first folio belong to Brutus. Sheffield interpolates three new lines immediately before this passage, "corrects" the original diction insignificantly, and also reassigns the passage—but to Cassius rather than to Casca. In his notes Pope argues for the transference to Casca on the grounds that the lines are inconsistent with Brutus's "mild and philosophical character," but he does not explain his choice of Casca as the more appropriate speaker.[22]

Inasmuch as Pope was obligated by long-standing friendship to prepare Sheffield's work with care, a possible counterargument is that, since his natural inclination would be to work some changes in Sheffield's play, he altered his friend's text after deciding upon the emendations of Shakespeare. But if this is true, why should he have left the Duke's "Stroke" in place of the original "cut," and why should he assign Brutus's lines to Cassius in Sheffield's play rather than to Casca as in his edition of Shakespeare? During the process of editing the Duke's play he determined, apparently, to impose its precise diction upon the language of a greater dramatist.

Meanwhile Elijah Fenton, Pope's assistant with the editions of the *Odyssey* and Shakespeare, was designing a tragedy on the lives of Herod and Mariamne. During their work on the two great projects the writers had maintained a friendly relationship. Inevitably Fenton turned to Pope for advice on his play. For over a year it occupied Pope's thoughts and correspondence.

Although Fenton's first mention of his tragedy appears in a letter to Broome of March 1722, he seems to have been at work on it much earlier. At the time of his letter he was hoping for a production in the following year. He first asked Broome for a prologue, which Pope promised Broome he would revise; but eventually Fenton turned to Pope himself. Pope, however, was unwilling to do more than revise, giving for the

first time the excuse that his anonymity could not possibly be preserved and adding that he had refused Sheffield the same favor.
The upshot was that Broome wrote the lines and Pope went over
them with care.[23]

Among Pope's suggestions for the Prologue, as reported by
Fenton to Broome, was one of special significance. He told
Fenton to advise Broome to stress Mariamne's imperiled virtue,
doubtless in hope of arousing pity in the audience.[24] Although
Pope had long since written his sentimental poems *Eloisa to
Abelard* and the *Elegy to the Memory of an Unfortunate Lady*
under the influence of the dramatist Rowe, this was his first
attempt to promote the pathetic style in the theatre. Though
only mildly reflected in the letter, his interest was to continue,
until ultimately he could give unstinted praise to so pathetic a
tragedy as Lillo's *The London Merchant*.

Shortly before this time, Pope had written to Broome, who
seems to have been his intermediary with Fenton, concerning
the possible production and presentation of the play. Although
Pope protested that "No man knows less of anything relating
to the seasons propitious or aspects favourable to the stage," he
set down some sensible remarks, to be passed along to Fenton,
on the advisability of staging the play at a time when many
theatregoers were sure to be in town. In passing, he remarked
that the play was "correct enough" (not in need of further
revision).[25] Apparently he never wavered from his position, for
it was later reported by Warton that "Pope thought highly of
the style of *Mariamne*; and used to say it was one of the best
written tragedies we had; and that the dialogue was particularly good."[26]

Although Colley Cibber had summarily refused to produce
Mariamne at his theatre,[27] seventeen performances at Lincoln's
Inn Fields were proof that the play was "correct enough." Nor
was this success undeserved. Fenton, in writing of Herod's un-
founded jealousy, did not step outside the bounds of neoclassical
propriety, but at least he attempted to characterize each member of his cast by individual diction. A comparison of the speech
of Mariamne or Herod to that of any character in Sheffield's
plays will point up the difference. For example, the funeral

orations delivered by Brutus and Antony in Sheffield's *Julius Caesar* do not present the sharp contrast intended by Shakespeare. But Fenton was intelligent enough to realize that character depends as much upon diction as upon action. Furthermore, he chose dramatic action whose turns were better calculated to arouse an audience than that of the usual tragedy of the day. His chief device, on which the denouement hinges, is Herod's arrangement for the murder of Mariamne after his death. Although Fenton cannot be given credit for inventing this bit of plotting, which is as old as the original story, in his play it provides a welcome element of suspense. By presenting this information through the words of the conspirators against Mariamne, Fenton caused his audience greater excitement than they usually received from the works of his contemporaries. To be sure, the play has its share of pathos—in the words of the queen as she demonstrates her willingness to accept her undeserved punishment and death, and in Herod's distress as he vacillates between jealousy and repentance—but the effect is heightened by the additional quality of suspense. Whether Pope was aware of this is uncertain; on the basis of his remark regarding the Prologue, it is safe to say that he was primarily impressed by the pathos of the tragedy.

In the four years following Fenton's success Pope apparently read no new plays in manuscript. Yet the drama was never completely out of his thoughts, for during the interval Lewis Theobald aroused his temper with *Shakespeare Restored*, an attack on Pope's edition, and the collection was formed of unfortunate lines which were to be burlesqued in the *Peri Bathous*. One letter written in this period is noteworthy for revealing Pope's judgment on dramatic diction. With more candor than he ever displayed in writing to his dramatist friends, he discussed contemporary drama with Lord Oxford in a letter of March 3, 1726. Many poets, Pope found, were guilty of putting high-flown language into the "mouths of persons not of the highest condition."

Nothing is so ridiculous as the lofty or poetical Style in such parts, which yet many Poets (& no very mean ones), are often guilty of, especially in our modern Tragedy, where one continued Sameness of

Diction runs thro' all their characters; and our best Actors from hence
have got the custom, of speaking constantly the most indifferent things
in a pompous elevated voice; 'tis not so properly Speaking as Vociferat-
ing. This goes even to their pronouncing of *Proper Names* . . . In
like manner our modern Poets preserve a painful Equality of Fustian,
throughout their whole Epic or Tragic works, like travelling all along
the Ridge of a Hill; which is not half so pleasant as sometimes rising,
& sometimes descending gently into the Vale, as the Way leads, and as
the End of the journey directs.[28]

This, it will appear, contains wisdom he neglected to pass along
to playwrights who needed it most.

The last of the plays to be brought to Pope's attention in
the decade was *Philip of Macedon*, written by David Lewis in
1727. If the two writers exchanged letters over this transac-
tion, the correspondence has been lost. The only contemporary
source of information is Lewis's Dedication to Pope, where the
playwright comments on the aid he received. He was grateful
to Pope not only for looking over the piece but for his "candid
Mention" of it, presumably to the managers. This was, apparently, the first instance of an attempt by Pope to persuade a
theatre to undertake a particular play. It suggests that Pope
was on good footing with John Rich in 1727, for the play was
produced at his theatre in Lincoln's Inn Fields. Apologizing
for the failure of the tragedy, which ran only three performances, Lewis continued:

It would be to no Purpose to insinuate, that a Performance like this
could be approv'd of in all its Parts by your discerning and consummate
Judgment; You thought not amiss of the most essential one, the
Conduct of it, and I had there my ample Praise. 'Tis admitted it has
many Failures and Errors, but if the Subject be not ill conducted, I
am sure, whatever I may deserve in the Sense of many of our Criticks,
I have in *Aristotle*'s and in Yours some Pretence at least to be for-
given.[29]

He concluded by referring to Pope's well-known willingness
to read whatever he found "to be wrote with Justness and
Spirit."

Although Lewis's Dedication is more fulsome than most,
and even shameless enough to compare Pope to Virgil, his com-

ments provide some useful details. Pope admired the "conduct" of the play; the word may be vague, but in all probability it refers to the action (that is, the events conducted), which proceeds with Aristotelian regularity. In this matter Pope's preference for the unities molded his opinion. The plot is in no way extraordinary for its day. Philip of Macedon has two sons, of whom Perses is the elder and Demetrius the younger. Perses, fearing the popularity of Demetrius, sets Philip against him, with the result that Demetrius is murdered. Philip, in the usual reversal of character, realizes his folly, but too late. In the focused action of neoclassical tragedy, no other solution is possible. By praising the quite familiar form of this play, Pope was merely repeating the opinions he had given other tragedies of exactly the same type. Whether the power of friendship was again at work is unknown, for Lewis left few traces of personal relationships behind him.

Thus ended the first phase of Pope's service as consultant to playwrights. By the close of the decade his admiration for neoclassical tragedy could be taken for granted, and he had acquired a taste for the pathetic. He had learned, in addition, that a manager might be willing to consider a dramatist's work on his recommendation. All this was meaningful; very soon it was to give pungency to the *Peri Bathous* and the *Dunciad*, where the corruption of theatrical taste and the strange ways of managers became subjects for grave deliberation. But the firm establishment of Pope's preferences in the drama was useful in other ways as well; soon he was to bring his judgment to bear on a series of tragedies designed to illustrate the struggle between Sir Robert Walpole and his enemies.

III

CONSULTANT TO PLAYWRIGHTS
(1730's)

IN 1728 Pope published the *Dunciad*, and the cries of the victims of that awesome poem pursued him into the new decade. The 1730's brought new preoccupations and numbers of new friends. Among the writers who began at this time to flock about him through admiration and unconcealed self-interest were Aaron Hill, James Thomson, and David Mallet. Pope's complex relationship with these three men resulted in his most intense sessions of editorship. For nearly ten years he let himself be flattered and importuned into reading their dramatic works while he served them also by transmitting messages from one to another and notifying each of the others' progress. Although he examined plays by two other dramatists during the decade, in the history of Pope's theatrical interests the 1730's are chiefly a record of his attempts to polish the strictly regular tragedies of these three men.[1]

The friendship of Hill, Mallet, and Thomson for each other was founded in their literary ambitions. Mallet and Thomson, both natives of Scotland, had been fellow members of an Edinburgh society called the Grotesque Club. Hill came to know both writers through their poetry, which he printed in his periodical, *The Plain Dealer*. Inauspiciously, a literary dispute brought Pope and Hill together; in 1718 they quarreled over Pope's derogatory remarks on Hill's *The Northern Star*. Ultimately all four writers came to see much of one another in the literary circles of London.

Of the seven plays which Pope read at the request of these playwrights, at least five were designed to support the political opposition to Sir Robert Walpole. Only Hill's were not directly involved in the prolonged struggle against the Walpole administration, but it is not unreasonable to suppose that they too contain allusions which two centuries have obscured. Propagandist drama had become fashionable, and these plays were only a few of the great number of tragedies attacking the court party. The writers of such works as these found the most convenient outlet for party emotions to lie in stage representations of Walpole, whom they repeatedly dramatized. Any stage tyrant immediately suggested the minister, regardless of the setting in which he moved. All dictators of the remote past were obvious choices for drama; with very little difficulty they could be made to resemble the "great man."

As the years passed and the Whigs became more deeply entrenched, they began to be opposed not only from without but from within their own party. A new figure, Frederick, Prince of Wales, rose to aid the Opposition. Resisting Walpole's influence, and resenting the curtailment of his allowance, he was happy to turn to the Tories and dissident Whigs for support for his patronage. In exchange, the playwrights among them—and these included Mallet and Thomson—furthered his cause with the theatrical public. How vital these matters were to Pope is not easy to estimate, but with evident relish he read and reread the plays as quickly as they were dispatched to him. If he had almost nothing to say about them as political tracts, he could scarcely have failed to interpret them correctly.

Thompson's *Sophonisba*, a tragedy remote from partisan issues, is the first play of the 1730's with which Pope's name has been associated. The two poets seem to have been friendly from the time of their first meeting, as Thomson demonstrated in 1727 by a warm compliment to Pope in his "Summer":

> Slow let us trace the matchless vale of Thames;
> Fair-winding up to where the muses haunt
> In Twit'nam's bowers, and for their Pope implore
> The healing god . . .

In 1729, while completing "Autumn," the last of the *Seasons*, Thomson also finished work on *Sophonisba*. Samuel Johnson's life of Thomson gives evidence that Pope may have written some lines of the Prologue to the play. Johnson recalled hear-

ing from Richard Savage that Pope had written "the first part"
but, unwilling to finish it, had left Mallet to supply "the concluding lines."[2] Although this is a questionable attribution in
view of Pope's distaste for such poems, it is not unreasonable.
Savage at certain times was friendly enough with both Pope and
Thomson to be a witness to their occupations. One might expect, furthermore, that Pope would begin but not finish the
uncongenial task.

Through correspondence with Mallet, Pope learned of
Thomson's progress with *Sophonisba*. Early in 1730 Mallet
reported Thomson's annoyance with one "Mr. D." who
claimed to have collaborated on the tragedy.[3] On February 28,
1730, a few weeks later, the play appeared at Drury Lane. It
received ten performances during the season, despite the bathos
of the much-parodied line, "O Sophonisba, Sophonisba O."

Meanwhile Mallet had begun to write *Eurydice*, his first
dramatic work. In the autumn of 1729 he sent Pope a manuscript of parts of the tragedy. Pope attentively read as much
as he was given and on November 1 wrote a well-considered
reply:

I think it a sillier sort of Vanity to undervalue one's Capacity, when
it can be of use to another, than to over-rate it, when it can be of none.
Therefore I would not decline your favourable opinion of my Judgment in Poetry; since what I have, be it more or less, is at your Service:
But it is no more than honesty to tell you at the same time, that in
Dramatic Poetry I am less than in any other. To say truth, I think
any common Reader judges there, of the most material part, as well
as the most Learned, that is, of the Moving the Passions: and you'l
agree with me, that if a Writer does not move them, there is no art
to teach him. As to the Particular Conduct, the Incidents, the working up of those Incidents, & the Gradation of the Scenes to that end,
as far as I can judge by the course of these first Acts, you proceed
judiciously & regularly. The Single Sentiments & Expressions are
surely generally correct, & where I can fancy otherwise, I will mark,
& tell you my doubts.[4]

In December Pope arranged to have the play delivered by
Lord Burlington into the hands of the Duke of Grafton, Lord
Chamberlain. The news that Pope was supporting Mallet began

to spread abroad; rumor had it that "Mr. Malloch's Periander [*Eurydice*] is much approv'd of by Mr. Pope, Dr. Arbuthnot and most that have seen it . . ."[5]

But delays set in, and several months went by before the managerial crew took action on the tragedy. In December 1730, Pope was rather annoyed to hear that Queen Caroline had received the manuscript along with a note that he had sent it to her. James Johnstone (or Johnston), a retired statesman close to the Queen but disliked by Pope, gave her the play, possibly with the hope that Pope would be placed in a bad light for favoring Mallet's political material. Writing frankly of his displeasure to Mallet, Pope reported that he had felt it necessary to make his position clear to the Queen: "that indeed I had read and much liked the Play, that the author was my friend, & that I would say, not only to her Majesty but to Men and Angels, that I both esteemed the author and his Work: But that I did not take upon me to Send it her . . ."[6] Not long after this the tragedy was produced. On February 22, 1731, it appeared at Drury Lane, where it enjoyed a run of thirteen performances. Pope, ill at the time with his chronic headache, wrote Mallet that he would attend the play if his health permitted.[7]

In *Eurydice* Mallet did "proceed judiciously and regularly," as Pope remarked—the regularity consisting of the usual timeless, placeless atmosphere. As Hughes had done in *The Siege of Damascus*, Mallet permitted himself some latitude in his interpretation of the unity of place: the second act is set on a seacoast, whereas the remainder of the play takes place in Corinth. Aside from this one aberration, upon which Pope made no comment, Mallet bowed to contemporary critical taste. The order of the incidents is normal: from beginning to end, scenes of pity and terror alternate with one another to produce the desired pathetic effect. In this familiar tale of a woman's trials and temptations, Eurydice, Queen of Corinth, is first horror-stricken at the advances of Procles, a usurper, then pleased to find Periander, her absent husband, still living despite rumors of his death, then again dismayed by his doubts about her chastity, then happy to see Polydore, her long-absent son, and so on until her inevitable death by poison. Periander,

too, is subject to the same risings and sinkings, until, stabbing
himself, he expires at her side. To the neoclassicist Pope this
procedure apparently seemed judicious.

The "expressions" (by which Pope meant "diction") are
equally unexciting. They are, in fact, cold and formal, as the
standard pattern of the play requires them to be. Eurydice during her moments of greatest suffering displays a philosophic,
calculated turn of phrase. Thinking Periander dead, she rumi-
nates,

> O night of ruine, horror, and despair!
> Walks there beneath thy universal shade
> A wretch like me undone? All-ruling Gods!
> Why have I lived to this?

Dying, she declares to Periander,

> Already death invades
> My shivering bosom. Yet a little moment,
> And I shall be with those that rest for ever.
> But here in this last awful hour I swear,
> By that dread world whither my soul is parting,
> I never knew pollution: I am still
> Your true and lawful wife.[8]

There is no accounting for Pope's taste for this chilly, un-
natural mode of expression, monotonous in its over-rhythmic,
continually falling cadences. To Lord Oxford in 1726 Pope
had commented that playwrights had fallen into the bad habit
of supplying all characters, whether of high or low position,
with language too elevated in tone. But if Mallet chose to let
his heroine speak in such a way, Pope presumably did not dis-
approve, for the dignity of her estate was unquestionable. It
would appear that a person of importance must be deprived of
all humanity in his speech, and any imitation of normal diction,
regardless of the attendant circumstances, was not to be allowed.
Neoclassical tragedy, the tragedy of restraint, hindered passionate utterance.

If it is to Pope's discredit that he declared such poor stuff
palatable, he can be absolved on the grounds that the play had
strong political overtones. It is possible to see Queen Caroline

as Eurydice, George II as Periander, Walpole as Procles, and Prince Frederick as Polydore. In such an interpretation the Queen is unduly influenced by the Prime Minister, who wishes to gain power rightfully belonging to the King, and the Prince is upheld as a vigorous opponent of the Minister. The King is thus warned not to neglect the duties of his position, lest the Minister preëmpt them. The politics of the day support this reading, for Walpole was indeed popular with the Queen, whom he used for his own political purposes at court. Finally, the appearance of the Prince of Wales as Polydore may be explained as an attempt to raise him in his parents' esteem. No wonder, then, that Pope was dismayed to learn that Queen Caroline had been told, with no foundation in truth, that he had sent the manuscript of the tragedy to her, for as political propaganda *Eurydice* was subversive. It is to Pope's credit that he explained his position to the Queen without hesitation, inasmuch as his professed liking for the play must have been taken as evidence against him.

While Mallet's tragedy was being readied for the stage, Hill and Pope were going through one of the several crises that marked their relationship. Since the first incident of *The Northern Star* they had bickered over literary matters. Hill in *The Plain Dealer* No. 16, May 3, 1725, joined the detractors of Pope's Shakespeare. Pope thereupon retaliated by labeling Hill a "flying fish" in the *Peri Bathous*, published in March 1728.⁹ Angered by this counter-attack, Hill brought out some unflattering verses on Pope and Swift in *The Daily Journal*. Then, in May 1728 in the *Dunciad* Pope touched off a spark with four lines which Hill took as a serious insult. The "H——" of the 1728 edition became two asterisks in 1729, and Pope added a note of reference to Hill's squib in *The Daily Journal*. After this series of petty bickerings Hill belatedly complained to Pope on January 18, 1731. Pope protested the charges against himself by denying any knowledge of the note and of the persons represented by the initials in the *Dunciad*. To impress Hill with his good nature, Pope even suggested that he would be happy to serve John Dennis, his worst enemy, if he could. Two more exchanges of letters in January and Feb-

ruary[10] left the matter still hanging, but Hill was clever enough
to suggest in them that it would be kind of Pope to read and
correct his poetry. In this way he enlisted Pope at once in his
service and paved the way for endless requests in the future.
Most of the dunces may have protested Pope's treatment of them
in vain, but Hill, as it turned out, eventually won a full measure
of revenge.

Within a few months Hill asked Pope to glance over the
manuscript of *Athelwold*, a revision of his *Elfrid*. On June 5,
1731, Pope wrote enthusiastically of the play:

Nothing but Trifles have I to object, and which were such as did not
once stop me at the first Reading; the Spirit, Design, and Characters,
carrying me on, without Stop, Check, or even Intermission. You certainly are Master of the Art of the Stage, in the manner of forming
and conducting the Design, which I think impossible to be mended;
of that Great Part, and of the other, the raising the Passions, I will
say nothing to you, who know them so much better than myself. I
would only point out a few Particularities in Thought or Expression,
as material as excepting to a Button on your Coat, or a loose Hair.
Two or three Lines I have with great Timorousness written on one of
your blank Leaves in Black Lead, half afraid to be legible, and not
without some Hope, that *before* you see them, they may be vanished:
So may, perhaps, my Objections, every one of them.[11]

Apparently Pope was sincere in this, for he expressed the
same sentiments to Booth and Wilks.[12] Hill was so pleased that
he asked Pope to look at *Athelwold* once again, and to make
some additional suggestions. Pope next offered to pass the
tragedy on to any others whom Hill might wish to have read
it. At one point he thought the King could be induced to read
the play, through the intervention of the Countess of Suffolk.[13]
A measure of Pope's concern may be deduced from the nature
of his corrections. He had told Hill in the letter of June 5 that
he approved of the construction but regretted some errors in
detail. Ten years later Hill used one of these errors as an example to Mallet, whose *Alfred* he hoped to correct. This was
the substitution of the phrase "and left but dust" for "by loss
of dust."[14] Two other corrections of diction were repeated by

Hill in a letter of October 29 which accompanied the manu-script on its second voyage to Pope. Pope had changed the phrase "shorten your meant absence" to "make your absence shorter" and had reduced "wishes" to "wish."[15] Hill raised some caviling objections to both these alterations, but his resent-ment was not great enough to prevent his asking Pope to read the piece once more.

With a rhetorical flourish Hill concluded his letter: "It is time to forbear persecuting you about this Tragedy. It is to come on before *Christmas*: But . . ." Here follows a request that Pope prepare a receptive audience. Pope made a strong effort to do so, as he informed Hill on December 9. He himself would be there, "sick or well."[16] Yet, after all the revisions, the pains, and even the attempts to command the royal ear, the work came to nothing. Only three performances are recorded—two less than the brief run of *Elfrid*, upon which this was to be a marked improvement.

Pope set down the failure of *Athelwold*, which he finally calculated he had read *six* times, to the "ill Taste of the Town."[17] But notwithstanding his generous praise, he had one telling comment to make: he confessed to Hill, after attending the first night, that he enjoyed reading the play more than see-ing it.[18] Here at least was a confession that Pope found the action dull. Yet could he have read through the piece—let alone see it—without feeling the heaviest boredom? One pos-sibility is that to spare Hill's feelings Pope had been overly generous with his praise. A present-day reader can only be amazed at Hill's temerity in allowing *Athelwold* to be staged. The plot is familiar: Athelwold violates a grave trust by marry-ing Elfrid, with whom Edgar, his king, is in love. Moreover, he has seduced another maiden, Ethelinda. Such a situation can only lead to disaster, and the path toward it is marked by innumerable stops at which Athelwold can indulge in the usual pathos. He questions himself on the extent of his guilt: Which of the three has he betrayed the most cruelly? Does he feel a renewed passion for Ethelinda? How can he accept Edgar's forgiveness? Finally, unable to live with such torment, he kills himself—offstage—while Elfrid, sensibly enough, renounces both him and the sovereign. Regardless of Pope's remarks, there is no disputing the justice of the audience's verdict.

In 1733 pleasant relief from his labors with tragedy came to Pope in the form of Robert Dodsley's *The Toy-Shop*. Dodsley, in the humble position of footman to Jane Lowther, had caused a minor stir with his early poems but was still a long way from the eminence he later reached as a printer. On February 5 Pope wrote to him in a remarkably generous spirit:

I was very willing to read your piece, and do freely tell you I like it, so far as my particular judgment goes. Whether it has action enough to please on the stage, I doubt; but the morality and satire ought to be relished by the reader. I will do more than you ask me; I will recommend it to Mr. Rich. If he can join it to any play, with suitable representations, to make it an entertainment, I believe he will give you a benefit night; and I sincerely wish it may be turned any way to your advantage; or that I could show you my friendship in any instance.[19]

Pope kept his promise, for Rich produced the little play at Covent Garden. Delays, however, prevented his bringing it to the stage before February 3, 1735, almost two years after the date of Pope's letter.

As a dramatic satire *The Toy-Shop* is akin to Swift's *Polite Conversation*, though lacking the Dean's acid brilliance. An essential difference is that, whereas Swift lets his characters speak for themselves, Dodsley provides an agent, the Toy-Master, who discourses on various manifestations of human frailty. He sells morality along with his trifles, and his customers visit him for his sermonizing as much as for his tangible wares. The Toy-Master receives a number of customers, preaches to all, wins their admiration, and concludes that he loves to preach as much as he loves to sell his trifles. Pope was correct in judging that the play has little action but was hopelessly wrong in doubting that it would succeed. It was a triumph for Dodsley: Rich accorded it twenty-four performances in 1735. During the same season other theatres began to play it, and it had frequent revivals in later years. Thus Pope must be credited with a major share in Dodsley's fortunes.

This pleasant interlude was all too brief. Hill, more fervidly theatre-conscious than ever despite his failure with *Athelwold*, was again demanding attention. Envisioning a future in which he might rise to the heights of managership, he began to look into the control of the Drury Lane patent. In the course of his inquiry he wrote to Pope on May 16, 1733, for some information on Killigrew's patent, which Pope had previously discussed with him, and within a week Pope promised to search out the facts.[20] Nothing came of Hill's attempt, however, for Fleetwood bought control of the theatre; but Hill's love of the stage remained constant. On November 7, 1733, he sent Pope a translation of Voltaire's *Zaïre*. Pope was to read it, express an opinion on it, and turn it over to Bolingbroke, who, of course, knew Voltaire well. Pope wrote a hasty reply, excusing himself with the comment that he was concerned over Dennis's sad circumstances and busy, as well, with a new poem Thomson had brought him. His only observation on Hill's work was that it was not only as beautiful as the original *Zaïre* but that it possessed the "Nerves" (strength) lacking in Voltaire's work.[21] As a critique the message is too hurried and too brief to be meaningful; it is only a compliment dutifully tossed to a man whose hands were cupped to receive it. All that can be said, or need be, is that Pope read the play. *The Tragedy of Zara* is no worse than *Athelwold*, but no better in its language and certainly no more distinguished in form. Nor, in fact, does it seem an improvement upon Voltaire's *Zaïre*. If anything, the translation is inferior to the original. The religious issues raised by Voltaire were all but lost on Hill, who was satisfied to present only the usual neoclassical pattern of rash behavior followed too late by mawkish repentance. As might be assumed, Hill found it difficult at first to interest the managers with such stale material and could achieve only an amateur presentation in York Buildings in May 1735. But in 1736 *Zara* was staged at Drury Lane, where, surprisingly enough, it received fourteen uninterrupted performances—a dazzling success.[22]

Like Hill, Thomson also aspired to fame in the theatre. One result of his ambitions was a benefit for John Dennis in 1733, of which he was the principal organizer.[23] It was for

this occasion that Pope, who intended to end the long contention between Dennis and himself, wrote his last Prologue. The
poem, already discussed, was spoken on December 18—only a
few months before Dennis died.

At some time in the mid-1730's Dodsley came to Pope with
a second play, *The King and the Miller of Mansfield*. This
gentle romance, Dodsley's chief claim to fame as a writer,
found a huge audience. When the piece was staged at Drury
Lane in 1737, it received seventeen performances without a
break and, in the suceeding weeks, four more. This is no sur-
prise, since the brief story of a king lost in Sherwood Forest
who sets all to rights between a pair of estranged lovers has the
charm of a folk tale. The crowds no doubt found something
else to delight them, too, for Dodsley's idealized rustics have
much to say on the deceitful ways of courtiers—their bribery,
their hauteur, and their obsequiousness. And who could know
more of such matters than the onetime servant turned playwright? Unfortunately, only Colley Cibber's suspect comments supply the evidence that Pope stood behind Dodsley. In
his *Letter from Mr. Cibber to Mr. Pope*, he recalled that Pope
and General Dormer appealed to him on Dodsley's behalf and
that, as a result, he promised to recommend a production of *The
King and the Miller*.[24] While Cibber can often be questioned
on his honesty, here he can be believed; for if Pope urged a production of *The Toy-Shop*, he very likely did so for Dodsley's
second play.

Much the same disparagement of the court was to be found
in *Agamemnon*, Thomson's next play, though it is of a less
bantering nature. As a disaffected Whig, Thomson had early
won the patronage of Prince Frederick. Following the strict
neoclassicism of Mallet's *Eurydice*, he adapted Aeschylus's
tragedy to suit the times. He had begun to meditate on the play
less than a year after the production of *Sophonisba*, but he did
not settle down to steady work on it until 1736.[25] When finally
presented at Drury Lane in April 1738 it received nine performances, thus allowing Thomson three benefits but scarcely
justifying the years he had devoted to it. To Pope, who was
active in the pre-production work on *Agamemnon*, the political

content was probably more impressive than the dramatic merit of the piece. According to Douglas Grant's explication of this *pièce à clef*, Agamemnon is George II, Clytemnestra is Caroline, and Egisthus is Walpole.[26] Agamemnon is very much to blame for leaving his country (to visit Hanover in 1736) in the hands of a guileful, malpracticing minister (Egisthus) who takes advantage of his master's absence to impose an unwonted tyranny upon a nation once free and happy. The urgency with which Thomson wished to make his point is obvious in a courtier's speech:

> And, on my Soul, methinks, that *Agamemnon*
> Deserves some touch of blame. To put the power,
> The power of blessing or oppressing *millions*
> Of doing great good or equal mischief,
> Even into doubtful hands, is worse than careless.
> Ye gods, avert the miseries that hence
> On him and on his family may fall![27]

This must have pleased Prince Frederick, who attended the sixth and seventh performances, and the Princess of Wales, to whom Thomson dedicated the published text.[28]

Such pointed matter could not have passed over Pope's head. He was taken into Thomson's confidence during the writing and was pleased with what he read, for, according to "Cibber's" *Lives*, he wrote two letters about the play to the managers of Drury Lane. These, unfortunately, have not survived, but some other lively accounts attest to Pope's enthusiasm. He attended the opening performance, and evidently his presence created no little stir among the patrons. The *Lives* continued, "As he had not been for some time at a play, this was considered a very great instance of esteem."[29] Johnson enlarged on this with a comment that Pope "was welcomed to the theatre by a general clap."[30] Going further, Charles Dibdin added that Pope "placed himself very forward during [the] presentation."[31] It may well be that all these writers were only building on each other's stories, but a vivid picture remains of Pope, with all eyes upon him, pushing to the front of his box. And even this was not all. When the first performance did not go so well as

had been expected, reported Benjamin Victor to Nathaniel
Wood, "a club of wits, with Mr. Pope at the head of them, met
at the theatre next morning, and cut, and slash'd, like dexterous
surgeons—the lovers are no more—and they have brought a
final scene, that finish'd the fourth act, into the fifth."[32] Surely
no friend could ask for more.

But all this was to no avail. On November 8, 1738, seven
months after the tragedy had its brief showing, Hill sent Pope
a long letter on *Agamemnon* which he wished to have passed
on to Thomson. All of Hill's suggestions point toward a re-
shaping of the play, primarily to emphasize the hero and to
remove some blemishes. Egisthus is not to tell Clytemnestra that
he plans to murder Agamemnon; Clytemnestra, because of her
immorality, should not be jealous of him; Agamemnon is not
to tell her that he knows of Egisthus's treachery.[33] These suggestions, if carried out, would render the play more "unified"
in the Augustan sense. Interest would be centered on Agamemnon alone, and the other personalities would be reduced to
shadows. Grim as the prospect seems, Pope professed to be
pleased by all this. He replied that he would tell Thomson and
added that the plan "is too good for me, with any Honesty, to
put upon him as my own."[34] Here Pope must have smiled over
this much ado about very little. Conceivably, he may have been
pleased by Thomson's pathetic treatment of Cassandra, and, in
all probability, he enjoyed the political allegory. But when it
came to reconsidering a tragedy seven months dead, he was willing to leave the matter in Hill's hands. The observation in
"Cibber's" *Lives* that Pope failed as a critic in praising *Agamemnon* is at least partially contradicted by the reply to Hill.

While Hill was hunting out ways to improve Thomson's
tragedy, he was also hard at work on a new play of his own,
first titled *The Tragedy of Caesar* (on Pope's suggestion[35])
but eventually printed as *The Roman Revenge*. His friends also
had new plays in progress; Mallet was busy with *Mustapha* and
Thomson with his ill-fated *Edward and Eleonora*. Pope, as
stimulated as ever by their minor woes, acted as consultant to all
three in what was his final experience in such activity.

It was Hill who exacted the greatest measure of patience

and time. In all, seventeen letters on *Caesar* passed between him and Pope. Bolingbroke, who was visiting at Twickenham, was also pressed into service. Hill first broached the subject to Pope on June 25, 1738, when in the course of a letter he casually asked for a "frank and friendly *Inspection of the Tragedy.*"[36] Pope's reply offers a measure of the care with which he and Bolingbroke went over the play:

I need not assure you in many Words that I join my Suffrage intirely with Lord *B.*'s in general, after a fourth reading of your Tragedy of *Cæsar.* I think no Characters were ever more nobly sustained than those of *Cæsar* and *Brutus* in particular: You excel throughout in the Greatness of Sentiment; and I add, that I never met with more striking Sentences, or lively short Reprizes. There is almost everywhere such a Dignity in the Scenes, that instead of pointing out any one Scene, I can scarce point out any that wants it, in any Degree (except you would a little raise that of the *Plebeians* in the last Act.) That Dignity is admirably reconciled with Softness, in the Scenes between *Cæsar* and *Calpurnia:* And all those between *Cæsar* and *Brutus* are a noble Strife between Greatness and Humanity. The Management of the Whole is as artful as it is noble. Whatever particular Remarks we have made further, will be rather the Subject of Conversation than a Letter, of which we shall both be glad of an Opportunity, either here at *Twickenham*, or in Town, as shall best suit your Conveniency.[37]

The correspondence continued back and forth, with Pope requesting permission to read the play a fifth time, and with Hill making over two hundred revisions based on Pope's suggestions. Bolingbroke gave some hints also, which Pope transmitted.[88]

By this time Thomson and Mallet were progressing well with their respective tragedies. All three asked for epilogues, but Pope, following his now customary procedure, explained in a letter to Hill of September 29 that he could not grant the favors.[39] When Hill replied that Pope's letter brought him his first intelligence of Mallet's play,[40] Pope thereupon became intermediary for all three. On November 5 he informed Hill that the others were not planning to stage their plays until late in the year, which meant that Hill had a clear road if he chose to hurry his work along. On December 8 he notified Hill that Thomson had written only two acts, that Mallet had finished but was willing to hold off *Mustapha* in favor of *Caesar*, and that, furthermore, Mallet was willing to smooth Hill's way with Fleetwood at Drury Lane. Hill, however, had no luck at all with the stubborn manager, and Pope, commiserating, wrote to Hill in January about Fleetwood's duplicity. Hill, although disturbed by his inability to interest Fleetwood, drew consolation from the fact that Thomson and Mallet were also having difficulties.[41]

At last Mallet achieved a small degree of success: his play was finally put on at Drury Lane. Pope went to the opening performance and, since the production was a matter of great concern to the entire trio of playwrights, later wrote his reactions to Hill. This was, Pope said, the first time he had heard the fifth act—presumably Mallet had shown him only the first four during the writing. Except for the performances of two men, whom he did not name, Pope found the acting disappointing. Even so, the audience seemed to react favorably.[42] Thomas Davies later reported that Pope sat in a box and was so pleased that he went backstage, "a place he had not visited for some years," and congratulated James Quin, who had appeared as Mustapha.[43]

Thomson, Pope also told Hill, was having such difficulties with Fleetwood that he had decided to take *Edward and Eleonora* to "the other theatre" (Covent Garden). Pope recommended the same procedure to Hill, but apparently in vain. The first three acts were all that Pope had seen of Thomson's play, but these he found admirable for their pathetic quality. Nevertheless, *Caesar*, he said, was still the superior play.[44] However, Thomson's greatest difficulties came from the Lord Chamberlain, rather than from the managers, for the play was suppressed after it had already gone into rehearsal. It was the second play to be denied the stage under the new law, the first having been Henry Brooke's *Gustavus Vasa* in the previous year (thus granting Brooke's play a place among the footnotes to theatrical histories which he might otherwise have spent the rest of his life trying in vain to secure). Shortly before the licensing bill was passed, Thomson as an Opposition writer had hinted his disapproval of it by composing an introduction for a new edition of the *Areopagitica*. His biographer believes that the Lord Chamberlain refused to license *Edward and Eleonora* through chagrin over letting Mallet's *Mustapha* slip by.[45] Possibly he reacted belatedly to the abuse heaped on Walpole in *Agamemnon*. In any case, Thomson had to take comfort in the proceeds of the published version.

In view of the patently meager quality of the three plays, Pope's curiosity about them is somewhat puzzling. Doubtless he saw *Mustapha* and *Edward and Eleonora* as political tracts and admired them as such. But why the patient, generous reading, revising, and rereading of Hill's *Caesar*? The solution might be that it was fun—an intellectual parlor game which England's most respected poet and most famous elder statesman, pencils in hand, could play in the pleasant summer air, passing the pages back and forth between them. But, alas, they did infinitely less for poor Hill than they reckoned. When they finished "correcting" the tragedy, it had become utterly unactable.

For surely "unactable" describes the printed text of *The Roman Revenge* (to use the title finally given the play), which presumably represents intact the *Caesar* which Pope and Bolingbroke read. Hill took Shakespeare's *Julius Caesar* and, like Sheffield, adapted it to conform with neoclassical doctrine. Although he made only one play, as opposed to Sheffield's two, and dealt only with the events leading up to and including the assassination, Hill retained Brutus as the central figure. Thus the early events of Shakespeare's play are stretched over five acts, to preserve the unities. To provide pathos Hill had Brutus believe for a time that he is the bastard son of Caesar, and the result to Brutus is an inner conflict between patriotism and paternal reverence. In this way the desired tension is supplied. Then, with appropriate delicacy, the assassination occurs off-stage. In addition, Pope's suggestion that he raise the dignity of the plebeians (quite inconsistent with the theory of diction he had set down in his letter to Lord Oxford thirteen years before) had the adverse effect of rendering all speeches monotonous in tone. These concessions to contemporary critical taste rendered the play so slow-moving and so dehumanized that no manager would risk it.

Mallet's *Mustapha* and Thomson's *Edward and Eleonora*, while certainly not stirring dramas, were at least worthy of attention as weapons in the political struggle. Mallet continued to honor Prince Frederick, his patron, while scoffing at Walpole. The plot of *Mustapha* is not unexpected: the Empress Roxalana, with the connivance of Rustan, the Grand Vizier, sets the Emperor Solyman against Mustapha, his son. The parallel to the domestic situation within the British royal family is obvious. Mallet deliberately emphasized the grasping nature of the vizier by having him confess his own share in several dishonorable actions.

Although he all but stood beside Mallet during the writing of *Mustapha*, Pope never committed himself to an opinion on it as literary art. It is possible, nevertheless, that he thought enough of it to contribute more than his letters reveal. Writing later in the century, Thomas Davies attributed to Pope the "more easy and natural" style of *Mustapha*, as compared to *Eurydice*.[46]

Thomson's *Edward and Eleonora* is more subtle in its partisanship than *Mustapha*. Whereas Mallet put Walpole himself on the stage, Thomson belittled the court party indirectly by vindicating Prince Frederick and his wife. In *Edward and Eleonora* Prince Edward, leading the English troops at Joffa during a crusade, is saved from an assassin's poisoned dagger by his wife, who risks her own life by sucking the wound. The pathetic quality, to which Pope always attached importance, is certainly present. The scenes of Eleonora's offer to Edward, his rejection of it, and her own mortal peril represent Thomson's attempt to wring the emotions while obliquely praising the royal couple.

One last play which Pope is alleged to have read in manuscript is Thomas Whincop's *Scanderbeg*, a tragedy not published until 1747, three years after the death of Pope and fourteen after the death of its author. Although the title of the play is familiar to most students of eighteenth-century drama, the play itself has not kept the name alive. The volume called *Scanderbeg* is less frequently consulted for the play than for the accompanying "Complete List of all the English Dramatic

Poets," which was the work of Whincop, John Mottley, and Mrs. Whincop. Mrs. Whincop, who saw the volume through the press after her husband's death, prepared a lengthy apology for the fact that *Scanderbeg* was never produced. Because two other plays had been written on George Castriot, the Christian defender of Albania, she had been unable to interest the managers in her late husband's work. William Havard's *Scanderbeg* she dismissed as unhistorical. George Lillo's *The Christian Hero* she asserted was plagiarized from her husband's manuscript, though Lillo knew she was depending upon the profits of her play for her livelihood. But, she concluded, *"having the Opinion of Mr.* Pope, *and six or seven Gentlmen more,"* that it was a respectable piece of work, she decided to publish *Scanderbeg* by subscription.[47]

It is, of course, possible that Pope never read *Scanderbeg* and that Mrs. Whincop used his name for its prestige value. Yet the play possesses many qualities that Pope admired. The attempts of Arianissa, Scanderbeg's inamorata, to guard her honor from the Turks provide the necessary pathos. Scanderbeg himself finally conquers the Turks and returns to Arianissa, but his near-defeat offers ample opportunity for raging and swooning on the part of the other characters. *Scanderbeg*, with its precise diction and regular action, is no better and no worse than any of the other plays with which Pope has been associated.

To the reader accustomed to think of Pope as the epitome of good taste in an age of criticism it may seem astonishing that he endorsed these tiresome plays. Yet the reasons for his doing so are easily explained. Pope seldom did more than give a pat on the back to an old friend—surely a forgivable offense. Moreover, in editing plays he could indulge one of his most persistent whims, to tinker with words on a page. From the early years when he was readying Wycherley's works for publication and on to the end of his career when he was revising and adding to the *Dunciad*, Pope revealed his passion for editing. Even in such important matters as the emendations of Shakespeare his zeal to remove imperfections showed itself. Furthermore, it is likely that much of Pope's praise was meant for the eyes of the individual writers alone, since many of the letters bearing his corrections and commendations did not see print until the nineteenth century and some not until our own day. Of a more critical quality are his *Dunciad* notes in honor of Gay, a playwright whom all the world might praise unreservedly, or, for that matter, the many other notes in the *Dunciad* on playwrights whom he condemned. And, to be sure, Pope's political interest, however small, is not to be discounted, for one of the basic assumptions of propaganda is that art matters less than persuasion. The modern reader should bear these points in mind before taking Pope's recorded taste at face value. It will be seen that, although he praised much, he found even more to blame.

IV

OTHER FRIENDS AMONG THE DRAMATISTS

THE aspirants to theatrical fame who came to Pope with their problems were only a few of his many acquaintances who wrote for the stage. In his sociable way Pope took pleasure in spending many hours with playwrights of every stamp. Whether in the company of engaging wits like William Congreve or disturbed personalities like Richard Savage, he apparently found some intriguing qualities of mind in all of them which bore investigation. The dramatists to whom Pope so willingly devoted his time and thought may be presented in three separate groups: the surviving giants of the Restoration, the writers of his own generation, and the younger men whose talents emerged after his career was in full swing. Although only a few of these men aided in Pope's intellectual growth, the names of most of them appear in his poetry, and some, as will be shown, stimulated his creative powers. His contact with each of them, however brief, gives a clue to the fascination which the stage held for him.

When quite young Pope became acquainted with a number of the older generation of playwrights—men to whom success had come before 1700. Wycherley, Congreve, and Southerne not only were friendly toward the young Pope but undoubtedly had some influence on his poetry. Pope knew the work of all the notable playwrights of the turn of the century, but he seems to have been on intimate terms with only these three. Towering over them was the great figure of Dryden, who must be named as one of the strongest shapers of his interest in the drama.

Dryden died at seventy when Pope was twelve. The two never met, but Pope claimed at least to have once seen his great predecessor.[1] He may well have had an opportunity to catch a glimpse of Dryden somewhere in London, and certainly he wished it believed that he had. In a lengthy appendix to the *Dunciad* he urged a comparison of himself to the older poet, and justifiably, since the parallels are many. In the uses to which he put his poetry and the form which he gave it, Pope never lost sight of his great forerunner. Also, like Dryden, in an attempt to insure his immortality—and his economic status!— Pope set himself the formidable task of translating a classical epic. Finally, both poets were Roman Catholics, although only Pope was born to the faith, and both contended with fierce enemies.

Dryden's influence on Pope was extensive and continuous. It appears not only in such obvious manifestations as Pope's adherence to the heroic couplet and his reverence for classicism, but also in his frequent and detailed references and allusions to Dryden's plays, which Pope read closely. On one occasion he confessed to Spence,

I don't think Dryden so bad a dramatic writer as you seem to do. There are as many things finely said in his plays, as almost by any body. Beside his three best, (All for Love, Don Sebastian, and the Spanish Fryar,) there are others that are good: as, Sir Martin Mar-all, Limberham, and The Conquest of Mexico. His Wild Gallant was written when he was a boy, and is very bad.—All his plays were printed in the order they were written.[2]

In addition to the plays named by Pope, his editors have found apparently genuine echoes of *The Rival Ladies, Marriage à-la-Mode, The State of Innocence and the Fall of Man, Aureng-Zebe,* and *Oedipus,* and others of rather dubious quality to *Tyrannick Love* and *Love Triumphant.* Still other allusions are to Dryden's brilliant criticism, the *Essay of Dramatic Poesy* and *On the Grounds of Criticism in Tragedy.*[3] The theories imparted in these essays informed Pope's knowledge of the drama as a literary genre. Unquestionably his tolerance of Shakespeare's irregularity was akin to Dryden's approval of experiment and innovation, for Pope excused in Shakespeare what Dryden defended in his own work. Yet, despite the praise implied by

Pope's close study of Dryden, it should be noted that Pope criticized him as a playwright for lacking "the art to blot" and believed that the language of the plays was sometimes either too high or too low for their content.[4] Added to the list of images and echoes, these observations provide a good example of Pope's exactness of judgment.

William Wycherley, only nine or ten years younger than Dryden, was Pope's first close friend among the playwrights. Despite Pope's vexations with Wycherley, especially those springing from his attempts to edit the old man's poems, he was able to criticize Wycherley's comedies soundly. Pope considered him among the best writers of comedy, in company with Etherege, Vanbrugh, Congreve, Fletcher, Jonson, and Shakespeare. Objecting to Rochester's complaint against him as "slow," Pope defended him against the charge privately to Spence and publicly in the *Epistle to Augustus*. He agreed with Spence, however, that Wycherley's style was generally stiff and added, "that was occasioned by his always studying for antithesis."[5]

At Will's coffee house, to which he was introduced by Wycherley, Pope came to know Congreve, who at the age of thirty had set aside his great gift for comedy and had withdrawn from the theatre. Although in semiretirement, the most lamented casualty of the theatrical reform movement, Congreve remained influential. It was flattering to Pope to receive Congreve's praise of his early pastorals, and he later commemorated the occasion by dedicating the *Iliad* to the older poet and recording in the *Epistle to Dr. Arbuthnot* that "*Congreve* . . . lov'd my Lays."[6] In the *Dunciad* he avenged an insult to Congreve's *The Mourning Bride*, to which Theobald's *The Rape of Proserpine* had at least once served as an afterpiece. It was the custom of the managers to put on the farces of Theobald and his ilk "at the end of the best Tragedies, to spoil the digestion of the audience."[7]

A third member of the crowd at Will's was Thomas Southerne. Time has covered over most of the evidence of friendship between Southerne and Pope, but in 1720 Gay included the playwright among the throng who welcomed Pope

on his "return from Greece," and as late as 1733 Swift wrote
to Pope of a visit from "our old friend Southern."[8] Since on
his eighty-second birthday the aged writer received some verses
from Pope in his honor, the friendship was at least long-lasting,
whatever its depth may have been. On the other hand, Pope's
opinion of Southerne's plays was never clearly expressed in
print; his single reference to them, "for the Passions, Southerne
sure and Rowe,"[9] is ironical in its context. A letter of early
1726 from Broome to Pope implies that Pope listened to Southerne read one of his plays aloud, in the company of Sir Clement
Cottrell and Broome: "Mr. Southerne wants an epilogue, and
will oblige me to write it. I am sorry he brings his play on the
stage. His bays are withered with extreme age. From what I
heard of it with you at Sir Clement Cottrell's, it cannot bear
water, and the lead of my epilogue fastened to the end of it will
add to its alacrity in sinking."[10] Presumably the play was Southerne's *Money the Mistress*, produced at Lincoln's Inn Fields on
February 19, 1726. Broome judged rightly; whether Pope
agreed with him has not been recorded.

To the first two of these men Pope's most widely read poem
owes much of its appeal. *The Rape of the Lock*, written at a
time when Pope was often in the company of Wycherley and
Congreve, is related directly to their plays through its theme,
characters, and language. It is as though the high spirits of
Restoration comedy, which the Collier controversy chased off
the stage, were harbored in Pope's spoof of contemporary fash-
ions and morals. The most obvious of the points of similarity
between Pope's piece and the plays of his friends is the fact that
the poem, like the comedies, has its *raison d'être* in the war between the sexes. In Pope's retelling of the dispute between the
Fermor and Petre families, the Baron, like Horner in *The
Country Wife* and Dorimant in *The Man of Mode*, is concerned with conquest. In *The Rape of the Lock* the cutting of
the lock is symbolic of a greater victory, and its meaning is
enforced by the outrage of a maiden no less furious than her
namesake, Etherege's Bellinda. Like her, Pope's Belinda is a
coquette. She belongs in the gallery of comic heroines whose
flirtatiousness is so predominant a trait of personality that it is

the governing factor of their lives. Her coquetry, unlike Mrs. Pinchwife's or Millamant's, is confined to the ombre table, but it flourishes there. In the game of cards the coquette triumphs, but in the surrounding sphere of life she defeats herself. In the comedies Etherege's Bellinda is furious with remorse; Mrs. Pinchwife is returned to the country; even Millamant's victory loses some of its brightness when Mirabell counters her demands with several of his own. Like those unfortunates, Belinda suffers a serious loss. Borrowing a psychological principle of the playwrights, Pope endowed her with the kind of personality that can achieve fulfillment only through a teasing hostility toward men. In Restoration comedy this is seen most clearly in Millamant and the London matrons who pursue Horner. In *The Rape of the Lock* the sex-antagonism takes the form of the game of ombre, and the loss of the lock represents the deprivation of virtue which the coquettes of comedy experience.

Accompanying the coquette and the rake are other figures whom Pope borrowed from his friends. Sir Plume, the fatuous blusterer, is one of Congreve's foolish knights now speaking poetry:

> "My Lord, why what the Devil?
> "Z—ds! damn the Lock! 'fore Gad, you must be civil!
> "Plague on't! 'tis past a Jest—nay, prithee, Pox!
> "Give her the Hair . . ."[11]

(CANTO IV, ll. 127–30)

In his support are two famous characters of comedy who could be counted upon to re-create the atmosphere of the Restoration. They are the most notable victims of Thalestris's wrath:

> *O cruel nymph! a living Death I bear,*
> Cry'd *Dapperwit*, and sunk beside his Chair.
> A mournful Glance Sir *Fopling* upwards cast.
> *Those eyes are made so killing*—was his last:
> Thus on *Meander's* flow'ry Margin lies
> Th' expiring Swan, and as he sings he dies.[12]

(CANTO V, ll. 61–66)

Appearing immediately before the climax of the epic battle precipitated by sex-antagonism, these two figures stamp the poem indelibly. Sir Fopling and Dapperwit meet "Death": an obvious pun, but one which suggests the consequences of sexual wars in pre-Collier comedy.

The elegant diction is another point of contact with Wycherley and Congreve. Pope was prevented by the mock-heroic pattern from allotting his characters more than a few lines of dialogue, but the comic irony in which he describes their affairs approximates the arch humor of conversation in Restoration comedy. It is Pope, not his characters, who speaks the famous couplets,

> Here Thou, Great *Anna*! whom three Realms obey,
> Dost sometimes Counsel take—and sometimes *Tea*
>
> (CANTO III, ll. 7–8)

and

> Not louder Shrieks to pitying Heav'n are cast,
> When Husbands or when Lap-dogs breathe their last,[13]
>
> (CANTO III, ll. 157–58)

but the style and effect are the same as that of the intensely brilliant drawing-room dialogue of Congreve. Mrs. Frail's speech, for example, glows with the same choice irony: "You are the most mistaken in the World; there is no Creature perfectly civil, but a Husband. For in a little time he grows only rude to his Wife, and that is the highest good Breeding, for it begets his Civility to other people."[14]

By way of contrast to the bright world of Belinda, Pope provided fourteen lines which describe the fiends, spectres, and animated utensils which inhabit the cave of spleen. It has been pointed out that these improbable creatures are taken from the devices of contemporary pantomime and opera.[15] In them it is possible to see Pope's comment on some of the theatre-pieces of his own day (a forerunner of the lengthier attack in the *Dunciad*) which differed so decisively from those of his early friends.

Less awesome than these older figures were the men of Pope's own generation, who, as the earlier chapters have shown, never ceased to solicit his commendation of their works. Among the most talented of them was Nicholas Rowe, a dramatist who, though older than Pope, produced his most memorable plays after Pope had begun to write. During the last thirteen or fourteen years of Rowe's life, when his tragedies brought him fame and the laureateship, he and Pope maintained a lively if curious personal relationship. Pope doubtless was familiar with all of Rowe's plays, although he referred in print to only four. If his estimate of Rowe's work was not so great as to suggest that his critical acuity was blunted by friendship, his recognition of Rowe's talents was far from perfunctory.

However warm their mutual regard may have been during the first years of their acquaintance, in 1708 Pope felt compelled to make a slighting reference to Rowe's unfortunate farce, *The Biter*. Irked to find that Rowe had produced a flattering introduction to Ozell's translation of Boileau's *Lutrin*, in which Ozell had written disparagingly of Wycherley, Pope recalled Rowe's most disastrous literary failure. Leaping to the defense of the elderly Wycherley, Pope wrote eleven sharp lines concluding, "How great, how just, the Judgment of that Writer! / Who the *Plain-dealer* damns, and prints the *Biter*."[16] Luckily, the lines did not see print until 1727, nine years after Rowe's death, when they were brought out by Curll without authorization. Yet Pope in scoffing the play did no more than restate a widely held opinion, for no one but Rowe himself found *The Biter* amusing.[17]

If Rowe ever got wind of Pope's cutting lines, he was not greatly affected; the two continued to be good friends. Rowe visited Pope at Binfield in 1713, to Pope's very great pleasure,[18] and the following year Pope contributed an Epilogue to Rowe's *The Tragedy of Jane Shore*. Although the Epilogue was never used, not the playwright but his leading lady, Mrs. Oldfield, was to blame for this.

Not long before the successful launching of this tragedy, Pope and Rowe found themselves attacked by Charles Gildon in a severe pamphlet titled *A New Rehearsal*. The attack takes the form of a tavern discussion of *Jane Shore* by Mr. Freeman, Mr. Truewit, Sir Indolent Easie, Sawney Dapper, and Mr. Bays, who are in considerable disagreement on the merits of the play. Freeman and Truewit, who call each other "Joseph" and

"Dick," were evidently intended to represent Addison and Steele. Although few writers dared mention Addison with such informality, Gildon, a Whig hack, could with impunity take any measures in maligning Pope and slighting Rowe, who was not overfriendly with Addison. Sawney, who is of course Pope, is supposed to have praised the play only in order to maintain his "Authority in the Disposal of Fame."[19] With no evidence to support him, Gildon relates in what sounds like the beginning of the myth of Pope's deceitfulness that Pope has written a favorable *Review of Jane Shore*, to be published by Lintot.[20] The truth is, however, that Pope disliked the play enough to speak against it to Spence. Rowe had admittedly attempted to imitate Shakespeare's style, but Pope, disapproving, observed, "It was mighty simple in Rowe, to write a play now, professedly in Shakespeare's style, that is, professedly in the style of a bad age."[21] Yet within a month of the first performance he quoted eight lines from the tragedy in a letter to another friend, choosing a passage to illustrate his delight in the country.[22]

Gildon also had it that Pope was in the process of writing a play about Lady Jane Grey. Recalling the remark later when preparing the "Testimonies of Authors" for the *Dunciad*, Pope added, "but it afterward proved to be Mr. Row's."[23] *The Tragedy of Lady Jane Gray* appeared in 1715, and although Pope had no hand in its composition, he was familiar with it. In a joint letter with Pope to Caryll, Gay wrote, "Mr Rowe's *Jane Grey* is to be played in Easter Week when Mrs. Oldfield is to personate a character directly opposed to female nature; for what woman ever despised Sovereignty?"[24] Thus Pope was up on the gossip of the production. But apparently he thought no better of it than he had of *Jane Shore*, for he quoted (incorrectly) a line from it in the *Peri Bathous* as an example of the imitative fallacy:

IMITATION is of two Sorts; the First is when we force to our own Purposes the Thoughts of others; The Second consists in copying the Imperfections, or Blemishes of celebrated Authors. I have seen a Play professedly writ in the Stile of *Shakespear*, wherein the greatest Resemblance lay in one single Line,

And so good Morrow t'ye, good Master Lieutenant.[25]

Unless Rowe confided otherwise to him, Pope was wrong in asserting that Rowe "professedly" wrote *Lady Jane Gray* in the style of Shakespeare. Whereas *Jane Shore* proclaims itself on its title page to be an imitation, the later play does not. It is possible that Pope, in a lapse of memory, confused the two tragedies.

According to Ayre, Rowe spent a week in the country with Pope in 1716, the year following the production of *Lady Jane Gray*. There the two poets discussed possible subjects for dramatization, and Pope made two suggestions to his friend. The first, a tragedy on the death of Charles I, was quickly dismissed as too recent an event. But the second, Mary of Scotland, found favor with Rowe, who said he would consider it. Pope "advis'd him to rescue the *Queen of Scots* out of the hands of *Banks*, as he had done the *Lady Jane Gray* before."[26] Nothing came of the conversation, however; Rowe thought the story of Lucrece a more suitable alternative, but death prevented his writing other plays. Only the image remains of the two writers in conversation amid the pleasures of the country, where the man of wit and intelligence offered ideas to the professional playwright in the hope of benefiting an art which he enjoyed.

Approximately a year and a half after this interlude Rowe took a step which may have imperiled his friendship with Pope. He supplied Cibber with an inflammatory anti-Catholic Prologue to *The Non-Juror*. Rowe may have believed that Pope was liberal enough in his religious views not to be offended, but the fact is that Pope had good reason to take *The Non-Juror* very seriously and not to forget it easily. When Pope, concealing his identity, hit back at Cibber's comedy in a mocking pamphlet called *A Clue to the Comedy of the Non-Juror*, his remarks took the form of an open letter to Rowe. While Rowe is not lampooned in the pamphlet, he is at least pointed to as partly responsible for the success of the play in his position as poet laureate: "I ENTIRELY agree with you, That there has not of late appear'd in Publick, a more *exquisite Piece of Satire*, than the Comedy call'd the *Non-juror*; or that better deserv'd the Distinction that was shown it, not only by your Self, as His Majesty's Laureat, but by all the Loyal Party in general."[27]

Pope's mild scoffing at Rowe's "she-tragedies" to Spence and in the *Peri Bathous* may have resulted from a memory of his annoyance with Rowe over the Prologue. It is true that in apparently sincere grief he wrote to Charles Jervas two years after Rowe's death that he was preparing Rowe's epitaph for Westminster Abbey, but the poem, when it appeared, chiefly commemorated Rowe's sculptured form for pointing the way to Dryden's tomb.[28]

But in spite of this somewhat dubious compliment and his unflattering remarks on Rowe's plays, Pope made use of the pathetic technique of the "she-tragedies" for two poems in 1717, the *Elegy to the Memory of an Unfortunate Lady* and *Eloisa to Abelard*. The influence of Rowe's style is especially apparent in the first of these. Like Lady Jane Gray, Jane Shore, and Calista of *The Pair Penitent*, the "infortunate lady" has suffered an unendurably cruel fate. The brief and vague outline of the unhappy times which led to her suicide is intended to evoke a purely emotional response. Writing economically, Pope set out unashamedly to reach his reader's heart:

> What can atone (oh ever-injur'd shade!)
> Thy fate unpity'd, and thy rites unpaid?
> No friend's complaint, no kind domestic tear
> Pleas'd thy pale ghost, or grac'd thy mournful bier . . .[29]
>
> (ll. 47–50)

No parallels to Rowe may be found in this, but the baleful tone and the accumulation of the emblems of death are his. One may compare them to the equally unfortunate heroine of *The Fair Penitent*, who pleads,

> Will you forget my Shame, and those wide Wounds,
> Lift up your Hand, and bless me e'er I go
> Down to my dark Abode?[30]

Eloisa to Abelard has been so frequently touched upon as reminiscent of Rowe that very little may be added to the comments of previous scholars.[31] However, parallels to pathetic tragedy in one aspect of the poem should be noted. In its structure, in which the cloistered Eloisa is torn between her undying love for Abelard and her religious intentions, the poem is consistently theatrical. In presenting her plight Pope attempted the play on emotions which such dramatists as Rowe were using as the pattern of tragedy. The reader of Eloisa's soliloquy senses his emotions to be clutched and then released as the unhappy woman sinks and rises in her passion. The range of action as Pope organized it in the poem exactly duplicates that of any pathetic play. The essential difference is only one of genres, for Pope was required by the form to present all the action, joyful and sad, in Eloisa's mind. A useful comparison once more may be made to Rowe's *The Fair Penitent*. Calista, guilty like Eloisa of an unchaste love, suffers unhappiness at the thought of her approaching marriage and then remorse at the knowledge that she has been the cause of great distress. The audience observes her pass from mood to mood as the play progresses until at last she stabs herself and dies. So too with Pope's heroine: her anguish finally reaches the height of fury, and, though she does not die, she thinks on death. Her story is presented in the conventional pathetic formula. There is, of course, no line-for-line correspondence with Rowe's tragedies, but the technique is the same.

Three less talented figures whose careers ran parallel to Pope's were Edward Young, Richard Savage, and William Duncombe. Although the fame (or, in the case of Savage, notoriety) of these men depended less on their skill in dramaturgy than on other matters, they must be considered here as playwrights.

Young, the most creative of the three, was in the outer circle of Pope's friends but close enough to comment significantly on the important turns of his life. The first appearance of Young in Pope's career was as an onlooker in the Addison-inspired controversy over Pope's *Iliad*. Having been intimate with Thomas Tickell at Oxford, he was surprised to learn from Pope himself that Tickell was preparing a rival translation. Later he notified Tickell that while Pope's translation was in favor at the university, Tickell's had a fair chance of knocking it down.[32] Pope, nevertheless, bore no grudge against Young for his championship of the Whig translation, for "tragic Young" had a place in Gay's *Mr. Pope's Welcome from Greece*. Later, when all Grub Street rose against Pope after the publication of the *Dunciad*, Young came to his support with two verse epistles addressed to him, both commending his offensive against the scribbling tribe.

It is reasonable to assume that Pope was acquainted with *Busiris* and *The Revenge*, the two plays by Young which were published during his lifetime. (A third, *The Brothers*, was withdrawn from rehearsal in 1726 upon Young's decision to take orders and was not published until 1753.) Although Pope never directly alluded to Young's blood-spilling, uncontrolled tragedies in his correspondence, Ruffhead cites an observation made by Pope to the Bishop of Gloucester which might apply as readily to them as to Young's major poetry: "Mr. POPE thought Dr. Young had much of a sublime genius, though without common sense; so that his genius, having no guide, was perpetually liable to degenerate into bombast."[33]

In all of Pope's correspondence only two letters, both of which raise several questions, are associated with Young. A letter from Young to Pope, dated only "May 2" and bearing lines from Pope's *Iliad* on its reverse side, has been taken as a request for a prologue or epilogue:

Having been often from home, I know not if You have done me the favour of calling on me, but be that as it will, I much want that instance of Your Friendship I mentioned in my last, a Friend Ship I'm very sensible I can receive from no One but Your self. I should not urge this thing so much, but for very particular reasons; nor can you be at a loss to conceive how a *Trifle of this Nature* may be of serious moment to me. & while Im in hope of your great advantage of Your advice about it, I shall not be so absurd as to take any farther Step without it. I know You are much engagd, & only hope to hear of You at Your entire leisure.[34]

Another mysterious letter, from Pope to an unknown correspondent, has been read as a joking commentary on Young's eccentricities, although Young is not mentioned:

My supper was as singular as my dinner. It was with a great Poet and Ode-maker (that is, a great poet out of his wits, or out of his way.) He came to me very hungry; not for want of a dinner, (for that I shou'd make no jest of) but having forgot to dine. He fell most furiously on the broil'd relicks of a shoulder of mutton, commonly call'd a blade-bone: he profess'd he never tasted so exquisite a thing! beg'd me to tell him what joint it was? wonder'd he had never hear'd the name of this joint, or seen it at other tables? and desir'd to know how he might direct his butcher to cut the same for the future? And yet this man so ignorant in modern butchery, has cut up half a hundred heroes, and quarter'd five or six miserable lovers in every tragedy he has written. I have nothing more to tell you today.[35]

The letter suggests a sense of tolerant amusement over gory catastrophes like Young's; and since Young had no equals in creating them, he was probably the man under discussion.

Another eccentric but less amiable man was Richard Savage, whom Pope met in the late 1720's. Savage had failed with two plays at Drury Lane: a comedy, *Love in a Veil,* in 1718, and a tragedy, *Sir Thomas Overbury,* in 1723. In 1729, as a miscellaneous writer with good Grub Street connections, he became useful to Pope in preparing the *Dunciad Variorum,* reputedly supplying Pope with whatever gossip he had on hand. When the dunces began to retaliate, Savage served as a kind of front for Pope in his rebuttal. Toward the end of his life, when his temperament and vagaries had cost him most of his friends, he still received encouragement from Pope. Living in Swansea in the early 1740's on funds which Pope and other acquaintances contributed for the purpose, he planned to refurbish his tragedy and reintroduce it to the stage. Offers to intercede with the managers came from a number of persons.[36] But Savage had sunk too far to act sensibly on the advice of friends, and within a year his relations with Pope had strained past the breaking-point.[37] Yet it seems unlikely that much good might have come of it had Savage secured a production; he was much too weak to refashion the play effectively. As a revenge tragedy, *Sir Thomas Overbury* lacks the motivation to carry it through five acts. If Pope actually read it, he must have been aware of the futility of any attempt to revise it. His chief concern, it must be said, was not for an improvement in Savage's play but in his health.

Innate kindness, so strong a factor in Pope's personality that for years he was unable to turn his back on Savage, rendered him responsive to the affairs of William Duncombe, who had been the brother-in-law of the unfortunate John Hughes. For a short time Pope and Duncombe corresponded about Duncombe's projected edition of Hughes's works. Later, when Duncombe's *Junius Brutus* was to go into production at Drury Lane, he sent Pope a manuscript copy, apparently with a request that Pope revise it for him. Unable to help, but wishing to give a kind word to the hopeful playwright, Pope wrote to him on November 23, 1734:

My Absence from home prevented my receiving your Two Letters till this day. I would else have read your Tragedy willingly: And I beg you not to take it amiss, that I return your present of the Tickets, since it is not in my power to be there next week, thro' indispensable Obligations in the Country at some distance. I think your Prologue a good one, & I think of Players as I always thought of Players, & of the Son as I thought of the Father.[38]

If Pope took the time to read the play, he found a love-and-honor plot in which Titus, the son of Junius Brutus, having to choose between patriotism and romantic love, makes the wrong choice and pays for it with his life. Pope's note to Duncombe is interesting only as a reflection of his attitude toward the Cibbers, father and son.

To the hopeful young men whose talents emerged after the growth of his own reputation, Pope counted as a critic and judge of stupendous importance. He became to them what Congreve and Wycherley had been to him: a great but approachable figure with the power to insure success. That Pope should find engaging qualities in the work of two of the younger playwrights, George Lillo and Henry Fielding, is especially to his credit, for they came to the theatre with verve, inventiveness, and an ingratiating disdain for traditional technique.

According to reports, Pope attended the first night of Lillo's *The London Merchant.* Greatly enthusiastic, he went behind the scenes and, says the author of "Cibber's" *Lives,* remarked that if Lillo "had erred through the whole play it was only in a few places, where he had unawares led himself into a poetical luxuriancy, affecting to be too elevated for the simplicity of the subject."[39] Time only deepened his respect for the play, for later on he commented, "Otway has written but two

tragedies, out of six, that are pathetic.—I believe he did it
without much design; as Lillo has done in his Barnwell.—'Tis
a quality of nature, rather than an effect of judgment, to write
so movingly."[40]

Pope's regard for Fielding grew out of literary and political
convictions shared by the two writers. According to a recent
study, Fielding's *The Author's Farce* (1730) reveals a debt to
the early *Dunciad* but ultimately provided Pope with the basic
structure of the *New Dunciad* (later *Dunciad IV*). In the
play Fielding dramatized the types of dunces described by Pope;
later the receptions of Queen Nonsense in *The Author's Farce*,
Queens Common-Sense and Ignorance in *Pasquin*, and Appolo
in *The Historical Register for the Year 1736* served as models
for the procession of the dunces before Dulness.[41] Pope's influence is easily discernible in *The Author's Farce*, where Fielding presents a dramatist named Luckless who is frustrated by
Marplay and Marplay Jr.—obviously the Cibbers—in his attempts to win a hearing for his play. Witmore, his friend,
gives him advice gleaned from Pope's observations in the
Dunciad:

'S death! in an age of learning and true politeness, where a man
might succeed by merit, there would be some encouragement. But
now, when party and prejudice carry all before them; when learning
is decried, wit not understood; when the theatres are puppet-
shows, and the comedians ballad-singers; when fools lead the town,
would a man think to thrive by his wit? If you must write, write
nonsense, write operas, write Hurlothrumbos, set up an oratory and
preach nonsense, and you may meet with encouragement enough. Be
profane, be scurrilous, be immodest; if you would receive applause
deserve to receive sentence at the Old Bailey; and if you would ride
in a coach, deserve to ride in a cart.[42]

Fielding followed up this oblique compliment to Pope with
a more direct one in the Preface to *Tom Thumb*. With a handsome bow to Pope, Scriblerus Secundus wrote, "The town hath
seldom been more divided in its opinion than concerning the
merit of the following scenes. Whilst some publicly affirmed
that no author could produce so fine a piece but Mr. P——,
others have with as much vehemence insisted that no one could
write any thing so bad but Mr. F——."[43] To be sure, Fielding

somewhat weakened the effect by making fun of a few lines from *The What D'ye Call It,* but once again Pope's writings provided ideas. Fielding's play, a collection of absurd lines from well-known works, is akin to the *Peri Bathous* and *The What D'ye Call It,* notwithstanding its burlesque of the latter.

For a few days in 1736 Pope and Fielding were linked by their common interest in the Opposition cause. Pope's partisan sentiments, though far from overpowering, were strong enough to give a political shading to the *Moral Essays* and the *Imitations of Horace.* In this respect Fielding is perhaps more puzzling than Pope; after producing a vigorous lampoon of Walpole in *The Grub-Street Opera* in 1731, he courted the minister with a flattering dedication of *The Modern Husband* to him in 1732. But by 1736 his choice was made, and he loosed upon the London stages a series of farces freighted with his contempt for the court party. In view of Pope's reputation as a friend to Opposition playwrights, it is not surprising to find a rumor that he attended Fielding's *Pasquin,* one of the bitterest antiadministration pieces. Fielding chose the old device of the rehearsal play to air his views on politics and the theatre, cleverly implying that corruption in the one was analogous to corruption in the other. *Pasquin* contains two such plays, a farce and a mock tragedy, each with a merciless portrait of Walpole. In the mock tragedy, the stronger of the two plays-within-the-play, Queen Common-Sense dies soon after the entrance of Queen Ignorance, who is attended by all the performers of popular entertainment. The hand of Walpole in the debasement of taste appears in the machinations of Firebrand, Priest of the Sun, who deserts Common-Sense for Ignorance. Ignorance, he says, is

> the most gentle, and most pious queen;
> So fearful of the gods, that she believes
> Whate'er their priests affirm.[44]

On April 8, 1736, five days after the first performance of *Pasquin,* the *Grub-Street Journal* printed a poem, signed by "Common Sense," in celebration of Pope's attendance of the play. On April 15 and 29 appeared denials of his presence in the theatre, but the rumor could not be put down. Ultimately, an imitator of Hogarth published a print of the opening performance with Pope conspicuous in a box.

The Licensing Act of 1737 strengthened the bond of interest between Pope and Fielding. It will be remembered that Pope's friend Thomson was among the early victims of the act. But Fielding, more than any other dramatist, was responsible for precipitating the act itself. His increasingly flagrant attacks on the court party, in which Walpole was caricatured with undiluted venom, led him into serious difficulties. It became impossible to ignore the outspoken criticism. Such farces as Fielding's *The Historical Register for the Year 1736*, produced at his own theatre in the Haymarket, and *The Golden Rump*, a lost farce by an unknown author, contributed to the high fever of legislative debate which ended in June 1737 with the passage of the act and the subsequent closing of Fielding's theatre. Pope subtly expressed his disapproval of the act in both dialogues of the *Epilogue to the Satires* of 1738.[45] Later, in the fourth book of the *Dunciad*, he spoke out more strongly against the new censorship:

> There sunk Thalia, nerveless, cold, and dead,
> Had not her Sister Satyr held her head:
> Nor cou'd'st thou, CHESTERFIELD! a tear refuse,
> Thou wept'st, and with thee wept each gentle Muse.[46]
>
> (ll. 41–44)

The passage may be, as Fielding's biographer suggests, a tribute to Fielding, for it juxtaposes a complimentary remark on dramatic satire to an allusion to the passionate oratory of Chesterfield in opposition to Walpole's legislation.[47]

Fielding is the last of many playwrights to whom Pope responded with sympathy and interest. Perhaps it was a mixed company of truly creative writers and opportunists too timid to travel beyond the familiar dramatic range who crowded into the pages of Pope's correspondence and poetry, but in Pope's view most of them made distinguished contributions to the literary theatre. Along with Hill, Mallet, Thomson, and the others whom Pope admired and befriended, these playwrights served as models against whom the intellectual dimensions of certain others were almost too paltry to be measured.

V

THE PLAYWRIGHT-DUNCES

OF the factors contributing to the decline of Pope's personal reputation after his death, none weighed more heavily than his asperity in criticizing patently minor writers. Choosing to ignore all evidence to the contrary, some critics have pointed to the mass of names recorded in the *Dunciad* and later satires as proof that he, like Atticus, could "bear no brother near the throne," while others have insisted that his sole design in these poems was the merciless pursuit of defenseless enemies. But these complaints, it must be said, ultimately prove ill-founded in the light of larger issues. While it may be true that many reputations suffered under Pope's incisive probing, others, by contrast, were made to shine. For by exposing incompetence, vulgarity, and corruption, Pope intended to clear the ground for the growth of moral and intellectual values.

The theatre, along with the other arts, was not to be neglected in the process; in all the satires it receives a share of attention, and in the *Dunciad* the lion's share. Pope observed that the general decline of taste in literature was in part the work of certain unprincipled playwrights. To save the theatre for gifted men he strove to drive out writers whose sole thought was for its commercial possibilities. Although some of the playwright-dunces may have been Pope's enemies, and intemperate enemies at that, their published attacks on him were less to be feared than their dramatic writings, which so cluttered the theatres that the plays of his acquaintances could seldom find an audience.

Lewis Theobald, the original hero of the *Dunciad*, was, after Dennis, the first writer to feel Pope's wrath. Nettled in

1726 by Theobald's *Shakespeare Restored,* which attempted to
correct the errors in his own edition of Shakespeare, Pope soon
found an opportunity for revenge. In 1727 Theobald produced *Double Falsehood: or, The Distrest Lovers,* a tragedy
which he asserted was revised from a newly discovered play by
Shakespeare. Although some recent scholarship tends to support
the claim, the general view held by Theobald's contemporaries,
including Pope, was that Theobald worked from a Renaissance
play by an unknown writer.[1] Immediately upon publication of
his play, Theobald became a subject for satire. All his dramatic
works, beginning with *Double Falsehood,* were scrutinized by
Pope for possible weaknesses.

In the *Peri Bathous,* published not quite three months after
Double Falsehood, Pope included Theobald among the swal-
lows, "Authors that are eternally *skimming* and *fluttering* up
and down, but all their Agility is employ'd to *catch Flies,*" and
the eels, "obscure Authors, that wrap themselves up in their
own Mud, but are mighty *nimble* and *pert.*" He added to
Theobald's embarrassment by printing three passages from
Double Falsehood. These quotations, chosen with discrimination and what must have been loving care, not only capably
illustrate certain sound critical points that Pope wished to make
but also ridicule the play. Pointing out the unhappy metaphors
to which "profound" thought can lead, Pope quoted *"None
but* Himself *can be his* Parallel." As an example of "Dark-
ness," which often appears in the metaphors of writers of the
"Profund," he gave a longer passage:

> *—Th'obscureness of her Birth*
> *Cannot eclipse the Lustre of her Eyes,*
> *Which make her all one Light.*

And, finally, he drew from Theobald an illustration of the
"BUSKIN, or Stately," style, in a passage which, Pope says, means
"Open the Letter": *"Wax! render up thy Trust."*[2] Through
carelessness or a lapse of memory Pope gave *The Double Distress* as the name of the tragedy in each of the three citations,
a confusion of the primary title and the subtitle. Angered by
this, Theobald wrote to *Mist's Weekly Journal* on Pope's ref-

erences to his play, including this error.[3] In subsequent editions
Pope corrected the mistake but did not remove the passages.
One wonders whether Theobald was mollified, in 1732, on
seeing the proper name of his tragedy.

Within two months Pope published the *Dunciad,* in which
his targets were the content and style of Theobald's literary
work, his professional standing, his personality, and—with particular emphasis—the scholarship of *Shakespeare Restored.* Unduly severe this denunciation may have been, and especially
when one considers that *Shakespeare Restored,* which gave initial
impetus to the quarrel, was more than fair to Pope; but as Pope
saw it, Theobald was free game because he had offended against
certain sacred canons of taste. For one thing, Theobald was
partly responsible for the success of such spurious entertainments as pantomimes and farces, which Pope detested. Moreover, he often engaged in the (to Pope) abhorrent occupation
of textual scholarship. In addition, he had done Pope the
fancied injury of providing a Prologue to *The Rival Modes*
of James Moore-Smythe, a comedy and author about whom
Pope wrote bitterly in the *Dunciad* and elsewhere. And he had
(or so Pope claimed) collaborated with Benjamin Griffin on
the key to *The What D'ye Call It.* Who else in 1728 had so
many black marks against himself? Cibber, who succeeded to
the throne of Dulness in 1743, had offended Pope in 1717,
but he had not yet become Poet Laureate, had not yet written
his self-appreciative autobiography, or embarrassed Pope with
an open letter. Nor had Pope by 1728 made the careful study
of Cibber's life and works which lent strength to the satires
of the 1730's and the 1743 *Dunciad.*

Another important factor in the choice of Theobald as
king of the dunces, and of Cibber as his successor, was the persistent concern of the *Dunciad* with theatrical matters. It is
clear, however, that Pope did not originally intend to blast
Theobald's reputation with the poem, inasmuch as he had
planned an attack on the dunces before Theobald published
Shakespeare Restored.[4] Because so many of the dunces are
playwrights and so much of the poem, including most of the
third book, is concerned with the stage, it seems likely that Pope

first focused his attention on the theatre—and literary commercialism in general—before selecting a hero. But the choice of a playwright as hero is significant, even though the playwright was also a textual scholar who had written the humiliating *Shakespeare Restored.*

Of the various aspects of Theobald's literary activity which Pope attacked, his dramatic work received the strongest blows. At the end of the first book the goddess declares that she has found someone to conquer the theatres for her:

> I see a King! who leads my chosen sons
> To lands, that flow with clenches and with puns:
> 'Till each fam'd Theatre my empire own,
> 'Till Albion, as Hibernia, bless my throne![5]
>
> (I, ll. 251–54 [1729])

Theobald, then, had one chief purpose, and Pope, accordingly, could not lose sight of his plays. Even when he mocked Theobald's scholarship, as he did in the notes, Pope persistently found occasions to write satirically of the plays. When Theobald lights the pile of his books as a sacrifice, only the plays burn before Dulness subdues the blaze:

> Now flames old Memnon, now Rodrigo burns,
> In one quick flash see Proserpine expire,
> And last, his own cold Æschylus took fire.[6]
>
> (I, ll. 208–10 [1729])

Pope, being careful to press his point, explained in a note to the passage that the names are from Theobald's *The Persian Princess, The Perfidious Brother,* and *The Rape of Proserpine.* Obviously Pope knew the plays well and had heard the story, admitted by Theobald himself in the Preface to the play, that Theobald had collaborated with a watchmaker on *The Perfidious Brother.* Pope went even further, at Theobald's expense, in the annotation of the line, "None but Thy self can be thy parallel,"[7] a version of the line from *Double Falsehood* quoted in the *Peri Bathous.* Here Pope had fun with Theobald's claim that the tragedy was Shakespeare's, playfully agreeing with Theobald but pointing out the need for several emendations of the text. Theobald's play and method were at once made ridiculous.

But, as the goddess's prophecy indicates, it was Theobald's efforts to undermine the theatre by writing burlesques that deserved the severest castigation. This was a man who despite his obvious ability in literature was contributing to the ruination of the arts, for, astonishing as it may be to those who think of Theobald only as a single-minded textual critic, he supplied the verse for nearly a third of John Rich's pantomimes.[8] Inasmuch as Theobald was a friend and collaborator of Rich's, he could be pointed to as one who had helped drive legitimate drama off the stage. In 1725 he produced his first pantomime, *Harlequin Sorcerer*. Because he continued the tradition of low amusements to which Elkanah Settle, the city poet, had contributed with masques and pageants, Theobald was Settle's natural heir to the throne of Dulness. Thus the succession was established through the medium of the stage. In fact, it has been conjectured that Pope's first design for the poem, before the appearance of *Shakespeare Restored*, was to satirize the selection and office of the city poet, whose duties were performed on the Lord Mayor's Day—an occasion not unlike pantomime in its empty showiness.[9]

One way to embarrass Theobald was to describe his work and its consequences, and this Pope did in detail. To give an example of what he considered the bad taste of the pantomimists, he offered two notes on *The Rape of Proserpine*. In this piece the authors required the burning of a cornfield, thus threatening the building itself in an attempt to satisfy the popular demand for spectacle. One such near-disaster could lead to another, and the managers of Drury Lane burned a barn on stage to meet the competition. As a climax to the poem in its original form, Settle, pointing out the sights of Theobald's kingdom, runs through the tricks and inventions which made up Rich's repertory: fabulous beasts, unearthly monsters, fires, dancing forests, whales in woods, dolphins in the skies, thunder and lightning, snow and hail. And often, Pope noted, managers degraded good plays by coupling them on bills with these offspring of "Tibbald's monster-breeding breast."[10] It is well to remember that until the appearance of the *New Dunciad* in 1742 the

highest point of the poem was the account of the decline of the
theatre under these circumstances. Although it is true that Pope
describes the pantomimes with such closeness as to suggest that
he was fascinated by them, he obviously intended the reader to
see the prophecy of the goddess come to pass.

In the early 1730's, when *Shakespeare Restored* began to
seem less important, and the *Essay on Man* and the satires were
in progress, Pope's quarrel with Theobald subsided. Learning
in 1733 that Mallet intended to print some unfavorable lines
on his old enemy, Pope suggested that the publication be post-
poned until Theobald's *The Fatal Secret* was staged.[11] Only
twice more did Theobald's name appear in Pope's poetry: in
the *Epistle to Dr. Arbuthnot* and the *Second Epistle of the
Second Book of Horace,* where he and Cibber are both mentioned.[12]

The juxtaposition of the two playwrights was prophetic,
for in 1743, not long before Pope's death, Cibber succeeded
Theobald to the throne of Dulness. With Cibber's coronation
the vigorous, long-standing enmity between him and Pope
reached its final phase. Pope, who was decidedly the more vocal
of the two, must be judged as chiefly to blame for their troubled
relationship; but Cibber, too, was guilty. Usually placid and
indifferent to all criticism, Cibber seldom responded to Pope's
outbursts. Yet at the beginning of the protracted quarrel he
played a part equal to Pope's in ill-nature. Before it ended,
with Pope's death, Cibber suffered a triple onslaught: Pope
attacked him on grounds of his dramaturgy, his acting, and his
management of Drury Lane.

The origins of Pope's contempt for Cibber are obscure.
According to Cibber, Pope never forgave him for coming upon
him one evening in a brothel; but it is far from certain that
such an embarrassing scene as that ever occurred.[13] And, although it is clear enough that Pope understandably found Cibber's poetry intolerable, the contention between them probably
did not begin over Pope's distaste for Cibber's literary work.
The affair of *Three Hours after Marriage,* recent scholarship
to the contrary, still appears to be the most convincing cause of
the quarrel. Pope struck the first blow figuratively if not literally when, hotheaded and furious, he dashed backstage to

threaten Cibber for making fun of his play. After this low-
comedy escapade the quarrel flourished.

Succeeding events indicate that Cibber was more annoyed
by Pope's backstage raillery than he later admitted. His strongly
anti-Jacobite comedy, *The Non-Juror*, which appeared on December 6, 1717, not quite a year after *Three Hours*, contained
much that was objectionable to Pope. The play, an adaptation
of Molière's *Tartuffe*, involves an English family who have
fallen under the spell of Dr. Wolf (the counterpart of *Tartuffe*), a treasonable Jesuit. *The Non-Juror* is thus an anti-
Catholic piece. As a Roman Catholic with close Tory friends,
Pope was certain to be displeased. But this was not all: at least
two and probably three of Pope's works are alluded to in the
play. These are *The Rape of the Lock* (which is quoted), the
translation of Homer, and "Eloisa's passion for Abelard." The
latter two are not specifically identified as Pope's works, but
are probably intended to be taken as his. It has been argued that
since *The Rape of the Lock* is unequivocally Pope's poem, then
any mention of a translation of Homer and of a work about
Eloisa and Abelard would be assumed to refer to Pope's. A
remark on the impossibility of learning Greek "in a month or
two," which accompanies the reference to Homer, may allude
to Pope's inadequate training in that language. Since it was
common literary gossip that Pope had undertaken a task for
which he did not have the knowledge, this reference would
have been understood by at least the more learned members of
the audience. The story of Eloisa and Abelard is mentioned
only casually, with no slighting overtones, but Cibber may have
intended to show the popularity of Pope's works in the home
of a nonjuring, Jesuit-harboring family—a case of "guilt by
association."[14]

Whether Pope felt the slurs or not, his many remarks on
the play reveal his displeasure. He soon produced the anonymous pamphlet titled *A Clue to the Non-Juror* in which he
pretended to discover that throughout the play Cibber had written ironically. Oddly enough, Pope later admitted on Cibber's
prodding that he had subscribed for six tickets to the author's
night.[15] It may have been, as Cibber thought, that this was
Pope's backhanded way of returning Cibber's compliment of

subscribing to his Homer. But it seems very likely that Pope wanted a look at this comedy in which so many of his works were made light of, for he must have heard about the allusions to them as soon as the play appeared, if not before. In addition to the remarks in *A Clue to the Non-Juror*, his later comments demonstrate amply that he did not subscribe to the comedy out of esteem for it. On one occasion he complained of "so damn'd a Play as the Non-Juror"; on another, he praised Lady Scuda-more for failing to attend it.[16] At last, in 1743, *The Non-Juror* was stacked on Cibber's sacrificial pyre in the *Dunciad*, where Theobald's plays had been placed earlier.[17]

After *A Clue to the Non-Juror* Pope dropped the quarrel for ten years, to take it up again in the *Peri Bathous*. There he found fault with Cibber's conduct in all three of his activities. Listing Cibber among the Parrots, "they that repeat *another*'s *Words*, in such a *hoarse, odd* Voice, that makes them seem *their own*," Pope mocks him for the lack of originality which led him to adapt rather than create. Cibber's prologues are decried, and his frequent stage appearances as a fop are ridiculed in a passage coupling him with Mrs. Oldfield, to whom also Pope was hostile.[18] Finally, in a passage charged with contempt, Pope leveled at the Drury Lane triumvirate:

HERE therefore, in the name of all our Brethren, let me return our sincere and humble Thanks to the Most August Mr. *B—t—n B—th*, the Most Serene Mr. *W—ll—m W—lks*, and the Most Undaunted Mr. *C—ll—y C—bb—r*; of whom, let it be known *when the People of this Age shall be Ancestors*, and to all the *Succession of our Successors*, that to this present day they continue to *Out-do* even their own *Out-Doings:* And when the inevitable Hand of sweeping *Time* shall have brush'd off all the Works of *To-day*, may this Testimony of a *Co-temporary Critick* to their Fame, be extended as far as *To-morrow!*[19]

Then came the heavy blow of Cibber's laureateship. To Pope this was insupportable. The event, which he probably foresaw, provided occasion for an essay and two epigrams in the *Grub-Street Journal*.[20] It also kept Cibber near enough to the foreground of the literary scene to make his repeated introduction into Pope's satires of the 1730's timely and appropriate. Cibber, in effect, was continually open to gibes. His name appears in three of the *Imitations of Horace* and the *Epistle to Dr. Arbuthnot*.[21] In this group of poems he receives praise as well as censure: the populace is held in contempt for disliking *The Careless Husband*, and Cibber is accused of breaking the laws of the drama.

Cibber suppressed his emotions through most of Pope's long campaign, but at last in his autobiography of 1740 he remarked mildly that he sometimes found himself dispraised in the *Imitations*.[22] He did not become irate, however, until 1742, when Pope published the *New Dunciad*. Finding his laureateship and management again reviled, he took revenge in the famous *Letter from Mr. Cibber to Mr. Pope*, wherein, vowing to have the last word, he took Pope to task for many needling imputations and sought to defame him by airing several disagreeable tales. Pope then set to work to depose Theobald and establish Cibber as king of the dunces. The resulting damage to the poem was not so disastrous as some critics have thought, inasmuch as Cibber had enough in common with Theobald to preserve the theme intact. Like Theobald, he had written poorly and in a variety of ways had contributed to the undoing of the drama. It is true that he had spoken out against pantomime,[23] but he had produced enough trash to equal Theobald's work in that field. In Pope's opinion, Cibber had, during his management of Drury Lane, capriciously staged dull plays while good ones went unacted, and as a playwright he contrived only to build on others' plots rather than design his own. Yet unlike his predecessor he was not able to accept the throne with equanimity. A second letter to Pope, imbued with his sense of outrage, gave him the final word which he had sworn to have, for Pope died within a few months of its publication.

The *Dunciad* of 1743, which combines the *New Dunciad* of 1742 and the three earlier books revised to accommodate the ascendancy of Cibber, stands as a summation of all the personal and literary trivialities that its author could not bear. The fact that Cibber is the hero is not as significant to the study of Cibber's reputation and talent as it is to the study of Pope's convictions of the acceptable and objectionable in literature. Yet it is possible to peer beneath and around the withering satire of the poem to find what Pope held to be true of Cibber and his works. Pope indirectly alludes to or mentions by name eight of Cibber's plays as well as his translation of an Italian opera and his adaptations of Shakespeare. Probably these represent considerably less than the total of Cibber's pieces which he read at one time or another. Above all, it is likely that he knew the ballad-opera *Love in a Riddle,* for a rumor circulated among the Opposition that in order to remove its competition Cibber had contrived the suppression of Gay's *Polly.*[24] Pope's treatment of these works ranges from a personal and provocative observation on Cibber's appearance in *Love's Last Shift* to a sweeping generalization on all "improvements" on Shakespeare.

Cibber's dramatic pieces offended Pope chiefly because of their unoriginality. The comedies *Love Makes a Man, Perolla and Isadora, The Non-Juror,* and *The Provok'd Husband* owed varying amounts to other playwrights. Among the tragedies of *Ximena, Caesar in Ægypt,* and *Papal Tyranny in the Reign of King John,* none was wholly Cibber's invention. In one blunt, brief passage Pope scoffed at seven of Cibber's adaptations:

> Here lay poor Fletcher's half-eat scenes, and here
> The Frippery of crucify'd Moliere;
> There hapless Shakespear, yet of Tibbald sore,
> Wish'd he had blotted for himself before.[25]

(I, ll. 131–34 [1743])

Pope also objected to "the *thick Fustian* and *thin Prosaic*" of *Perolla and Isadora, Caesar in Ægypt,* and *Ximena.*[26] Just one play was admitted to be good: "Some Dæmon stole my pen (forgive th'offence) / And once betray'd me into common sense."[27] Probably Pope was once again confessing a qualified admiration for *The Careless Husband*; ironically, he hinted that Cibber might not have written it.[28]

In all, the number of Cibber's pieces that Pope demonstrably knew is thirteen, or half the total. The logical inference, supported by the passages on *The Careless Husband,* is that Pope was not merely airing a series of grudges, despite his animosity, but, rather, that after a careful study of Cibber's works he became convinced of their worthlessness. One might argue today that Cibber's plays hardly deserved such treatment, since they have stood up far better than the plays of most of his contemporaries; but Pope's attitude is understandable. In the light of this interpretation of his criticism, the *Dunciad* becomes an eloquent defense of the theatre against men who were debasing it by their works.

Many other playwright-dunces felt the heat of Pope's fury. Those who received special attention were Thomas Cooke, Charles Johnson, James Ralph, and James Moore-Smythe. Pope took issue with a larger group of playwrights on more grounds than their plays alone. These, in the order of appearance in the *Dunciad*, were Ambrose Philips, John Oldmixon, Mrs. Centlivre, Mrs. Heywood, William Popple, and Leonard Welsted. The list is long, but it is perhaps worth noting that of all these dramatists only Mrs. Centlivre might be spared.

The fact that Pope chose other reasons for quarreling with these scribblers has obscured the soundness of his criticism of their wretched plays. He was invariably honest, however, in his opinions of them as playwrights. When, for instance, Pope took "Hesiod" Cooke to task for the poor quality of his ballad-opera *Penelope,* mistakenly believing that Cooke and not John Mottley had the major share in it, his reason was that the piece foolishly burlesqued a noble poem, the *Odyssey*; the fact that his own translation was obliquely involved in the parody was secondary—farce and epic combined in the play to "get a jumbled race."[29] In similar fashion Pope complained of Charles Johnson as an unoriginal writer.[30] The charge was nonetheless honest for being in keeping with the early falling out between them, when Johnson upheld adaptations in the face of Pope's dislike for them. Johnson took the dispute to heart; in a foreword to *The Tragedy of Medea,* his post-*Dunciad* adaptation of Euripides, he blamed Pope for the damning of his play and sardonically warned other playwrights to show proper humility to Pope "before the curtain goes up."[31] Nor did Pope exaggerate in his criticism of James Ralph: "He was wholly illiterate, and knew no Language, not even *French*: Being advised to read the Rules of Dramatick Poetry before he began a Play, he smiled and reply'd, *Shakespear writ without Rules*."[32] Although Pope did not include Ralph in the *Dunciad* until the appearance of his *Sawney,* which Pope accurately described as a "Swearing-piece," the comment stands independent of the rancor which motivated Pope to write it.

Of the minor figures, James Moore-Smythe was undoubtedly the most offensive to Pope. The scornful remarks on this would-be playwright in the *Dunciad* and elsewhere are the result of Pope's unhappiest experience in the theatre. After inserting six unpublished lines by Pope in his absurd comedy of humors, *The Rival Modes*, apparently with Pope's permission, he then—or so Pope asserted in the *Dunciad*—was foolish enough to request Pope not to reclaim them.[33] Unwilling to grant this favor, Pope then printed them in the "last" volume of the *Miscellanies*, where they appear in "To Mrs. M. B. Sent on Her Birth-Day."[34] So uncontrolled was his rage that Pope bluntly labeled Moore-Smythe a plagiarist and explained the incident in full. His charge is insubstantial, however, for the lines were clearly intended by Moore-Smythe to appear as a quotation and are shortly followed by a line from the *Essay on Criticism*.[35] In all probability Pope hoped to indicate his displeasure in being held in any way responsible for so poor a comedy as *The Rival Modes*, which deservedly received no more than six performances at Drury Lane. Remembering the incident as late as 1735, Pope wrote in the *Epistle to Dr. Arbuthnot* that Moore-Smythe "neglects the laws."[36] Inasmuch as comedy had no "laws," in the sense that tragedy had them— unless, of course, Pope had in mind the laws against plagiarism —the charge is meaningless. It is as though the words came out by reflex action as he recalled the insipid play.

In his troubled relationship with this inept dramatist, the last of the playwright-dunces to rouse his temper, Pope gave evidence once again of his high regard for theatrical art. Whether dispatching so feeble an adversary as Moore-Smythe or cautiously revealing the inanities of a Theobald or Cibber, Pope never forgot his purpose—the defense of intellectual theatre. But the defense was not an easy one to maintain, and its futility may best be revealed by the fact that the first and final versions of the *Dunciad*, though written fifteen years apart, register the same protests. Abetted by managers and audiences, too many writers were content to abandon art for the comforts of commercial success.

VI

ACTORS, MANAGERS, AND AUDIENCE

WHILE observing the difficulties of Fenton, Hill, and Mallet in placing their tragedies, Pope learned that the well-being of the theatre was as much dependent upon responsible actors and managers as upon conscientious writers, and that these groups in turn were subject to the demands of often capricious audiences. In Pope's view all were in need of correction, for all conspired to cheapen the stage. At the same time that he reminded the dramatists of their duties toward the public, he railed against the actors, managers, and public itself for the nonsense which they offered and accepted in the name of theatre. Moreover, he pronounced them guilty of an offense which only a few of the writers committed: they were morally irresponsible. In the wantonness of the private lives of actors and the commercialism of managers Pope saw their ineptness for the theatrical profession, and in the deplorable taste and manners of the audience he detected a frivolous disregard for literary art which went hand in hand with the dissolution of social standards.

Pope's dissatisfaction with these groups grew slowly but steadily. Only on rare occasions did he look on the professionals with a friendly eye. In his youth he had associated freely with the actors Thomas Betterton and Mrs. Bicknell, but Gay's verse epistle, *Mr. Pope's Welcome from Greece*, presumably written in 1720, contains the last references to people of the theatre as Pope's friends. Although relations were seldom as strained as he liked to pretend in his poetry and letters, where he professed to be completely alienated, he was in his later years not actually friendly toward them as a class or as individuals. By 1728, with the publication of the *Peri Bathous*, Pope viewed them only as performers or as men who could serve him in a few special capacities. In the *Dunciad* and the poems which followed it, players and managers alike were evidently considered outside the pale, while the audience, with its lack of discrimination in entertainment and lack of decorum in public behavior, deserved to be labeled the "many-headed Monster of the Pit."[1]

Of these groups, the actors were Pope's most obvious targets. They were public figures whom anyone might see nightly in the theatre or read about almost daily in libelous pamphlets. The scandals surrounding their names were endless, and these offended Pope as much as did their efforts in collaboration with managers to turn the theatre into an arena for spectacle. In part it was the twofold error of their ways—delinquency added to commercialism—that allowed Pope to criticize them where he could forgive or ignore the morally dubious actions of his intimates. He showed no alarm over the relationship of his friend Congreve with a married duchess, for example, and he never alluded to Bolingbroke's succession of mistresses. But these were gentlemen—intelligent men, in fact—who had the good sense to conceal their affairs. Actors, however, were gentlemen and ladies only when playing parts on the stage, and too often the parts were not worth playing. Although frequently it was possible for Pope to praise the brilliant interpretation of a role, great acting alone did not always redeem a performer in his eyes, for often a fine actor joined forces with a producer of low taste. To register his contempt for the actors' part in the vulgarization of the stage, Pope seized upon their personal lives as evidence of their lack of discretion.

Early in his life, before the moral note in his poetry became strong, Pope was on good terms with a number of distinguished players, including the actresses Barry, Bicknell, Younger, and Santlow, and the great actors Thomas Betterton and Barton Booth. Presumably he was well acquainted with the entire casts of *Cato*, *The What D'ye Call It*, and *Three Hours*, but his only intimates among them, so far as is known, were the sisters Bicknell and Younger. It is likely that Thomas Betterton was Pope's only close friend among the actors. Pope painted a portrait of him and helped him with some modernizations of Chaucer.[2] At one time considering him the best actor he had seen, Pope was willing to concede that "in Betterton's days the older sort of people talked of Harte's being his superior, just as we do of Betterton's being the superior to those now."[3]

How well Pope knew Elizabeth Barry is uncertain, although it is unlikely that he could have seen Betterton often without encountering the actress in his company. The only authority, however, for including her among Pope's theatrical acquaintances is a remark addressed to him by Bolingbroke in his *Essay the Fourth, Concerning Authority in Matters of Religion*: "You and I knew Betterton and Mrs. Barry off the stage as well as on it, and yet I am persuaded neither of us could ever see Jaffeir and Belvidera without horrour and compassion."[4] On slim evidence it has been suggested that Mrs. Barry was for a time the mistress of Bolingbroke's father.[5] Pope may have seen Betterton and Mrs. Barry together in Congreve's *Love for Love* on April 7, 1709, when the actress returned after two years' semi-retirement to play Mrs. Frail in Betterton's benefit.[6] But this is mere conjecture. If Pope knew her personally or saw her in *Venice Preserv'd*, as Bolingbroke assumed, he never wrote about it.

More is known about Pope's acquaintance with Mrs. Bicknell,[7] Elizabeth Younger, and Hester Santlow. The sisters Bicknell and Younger appeared as Kitty and Joyce respectively in *The What D'ye Call It*, and two seasons later Bicknell played the part of Phoebe Clinket in *Three Hours after Marriage*. Pope took delight in their society, as evidenced by his playful reference to them in *A Farewell to London. In the Year 1715*:

> My Friends, by Turns, my Friends confound,
>   Betray, and are betray'd:
> Poor Y——r's sold for Fifty Pound,
>   And B——ll is a Jade.[8]

> (ll. 29–32)

Unfortunately, the lines are obscure. The poem, which expresses Pope's mingled joy and regret on leaving London for the hard task of translating Homer in the country, lumps together in delightful confusion all those pleasures and distractions which make steady concentration impossible in the city. Younger and Bicknell were a part of London life for Pope, but who betrayed them or was betrayed by them it is impossible to say. Perhaps Pope was merely mocking himself for giving up such an amusing pair for his money-making translation. In any event, the young women were still among Pope's friends in 1720, when they appeared in Gay's epistle as "frolick Bicknell, and her sister young." But after this there are no more references to them.

Barton Booth and Hester Santlow, husband and wife, were also mentioned in Gay's poem. Although Pope railed against Booth's management of Drury Lane, he was usually kind in his references to the actor. In 1731 he cautioned Hill to postpone *Athelwold* until Booth and Mrs. Porter, both indisposed, should be well enough to appear, and six years later in the *Epistle to Augustus* he wrote of "well-mouth'd Booth."[9]

It was in quite another vein that Pope wrote of Ann Oldfield, Colley Cibber's children, and John Rich. Granting them places in his poems because of their failure to support what he considered intellectual drama, Pope reminded the public of their offstage misdeeds.

None received more careful attention than Mrs. Oldfield, who was associated in his mind with Cibber, king of the dunces. Possibly because she declined to speak his Epilogue to Rowe's *Jane Shore*, or, if Breval wrote truthfully in *The Confederates*, because she refused to continue in *Three Hours after Marriage*, Pope drew her character in his blackest ink. In addition to the early squib in the aftermath of *Cato* (only tentatively attributed to Pope) are references to her in two poems written after her death. In the *Epistle to Cobham* she delivers a deathbed monologue:

> "Odious! in woolen! 'twould a Saint provoke,
> (Were the last words that poor Narcissa spoke)
> "No, let a charming Chintz, and Brussels lace
> "Wrap my cold limbs, and shade my lifeless face:
> "One would not, sure, be frightful when one's dead—
> "And—Betty—give this Cheek a little Red."[10]

(ll. 242–47)

Mrs. Oldfield is easily identified as the speaker, for she frequently played Narcissa in Cibber's *Love's Last Shift*; possibly Pope gives a clue to his motives by naming her after one of Cibber's characters. As the poem relates, Mrs. Oldfield had been buried not in wool, as the law required, but in lace and a winding sheet. The Betty of the poem is another actress, Margaret Saunders, who had been a confidante of Mrs. Oldfield and had prepared her body for burial.[11] In *Sober Advice from Horace* the actress became "Engaging *Oldfield!* who, with Grace and Ease, / Could joyn the Arts, to ruin, and to please."[12] Here it would appear that Pope despised her for using her talent as an actress only for improper purposes. Indeed, all the allusions combine to give a picture of a petty, extravagant, immoral woman, doubtless as Pope intended.

No less meretricious were Colley Cibber's son and daughter, Theophilus Cibber and Charlotte Cibber Charke. Undeniably, what Pope repeated about their moral improvidence was true: they were creatures to contemplate with awe and wonder. Theophilus, less than a shadow of his father as a craftsman, shocked the literary and theatrical worlds by acting as pander for his wife, Susannah Marie Arne. Charlotte, perhaps even odder than her brother, entered the theatre only to leave it for a life of extraordinary escapades.[13] With such examples as these before him, not only dissolute in private life but tainted as well by their father's vulgar taste, Pope had no trouble in condemning actors as a class. In the first version of the *Dunciad* he predicted Theophilus's grotesque career:

> "Mark first the youth who takes the foremost place,
> And thrusts his person full into your face.
> With all thy Father's virtues blest, be born!
> And a new Cibber shall the Stage adorn.[14]

> (III, ll. 131–34 [1729])

In the later version, when the prophecy had come to pass, he forced their father to tell the truth about them while praying over the ashes of his books:

> "O born in sin, and forth in folly brought!
> Works damn'd, or to be damn'd (your father's fault)

Go, purify'd by flames ascend the sky,
My better and more christian progeny!
Unstain'd, untouch'd, and yet in maiden sheets;
While all your smutty sisters walk the streets.[15]

(I, ll. 225–30 [1743])

The personal life of John Rich drew brief but pungent comment: "Ye Gods! shall *Cibber*'s Son, without rebuke / Swear like a Lord? or *Rich* out-whore a Duke?"[16] Unpleasant as the imputation may be, it was made worse by association with the disreputable Theophilus. But it was Rich's professional life that embittered Pope. The considerable detail he lavished on Rich's stagecraft in the *Dunciad* suggests that he may have enjoyed the performances, but there is no disputing the fact that Pope intended to decry them for keeping serious works out of the theatre. As both actor and manager Rich was to blame for such low-brow displays. For the same reason in the *Epistle to Augustus* Pope struck at William Pinkethman, who catered to the mob in one of Cibber's comedies by consuming two chickens on stage.[17]

Pope's general remarks were as bitter as these personal condemnations. To Spence he confided his principal reason for refusing to write tragedy: "I had taken such strong resolutions against anything of that kind from seeing how much everybody that did write for the stage, was obliged to subject themselves to the players and the town."[18] To understand how objectionable the actors were to him, one must turn to the "Project for the Advancement of the Stage" in the *Peri Bathous*, where he links their moral abandon to their indifference toward art. Promiscuous actresses, Pope recommends, should be penalized if their laxity results in calamity: "IF it be discover'd that any Actress is got with Child, during the Interludes of any Play, wherein she hath a part, it shall be reckon'd a neglect of her Business, and she shall *forfeit* accordingly."[19] More subtle than this, another method of exposing them was to suggest that all actresses appeared in pantomimes as well as in plays and were therefore practitioners of a low craft, as in *Sober Advice from Horace*:

> To *Palmer*'s Bed no Actress comes amiss,
> He courts the whole *Personae Dramatis:*
> He too can say, "With Wives I never sin."
> But Singing-Girls and Mimicks draw him in.[20]

(ll. 71–74)

No doubt Pope's convictions were confirmed in 1735 by the willingness of James Worsdale to assist him with the duping of Curll into bringing out an edition of his correspondence with Swift in order that an "authentic" edition might be presented later. Worsdale, a theatrical hanger-on whom Mrs. Thrale uncompromisingly labeled "the Pimp," served as go-between for "P.T." (Pope) and Curll during the proceedings.[21] Wishing to transact quite dubious business, Pope probably chose this reprobate because the job required the talents of a man who could act.

But the severity of Pope's criticism must be counterbalanced by his hearty praise of actors whose professional skill he admired and whose private lives were above reproach. The backstage visits to Quin after his performance in *Mustapha* and to the cast of *The London Merchant* were generous gestures, and other reports tell of even greater expansiveness. One anecdote, possibly apocryphal, concerns Pope in the audience for Charles Macklin's Shylock in 1741. According to James Thomas Kirkman, Macklin's biographer, Pope was so overcome by delight that he rose in his stage box and "emphatically exclaimed—

> This is the Jew
> That SHAKESPEARE drew."[22]

The story was presented for the first time in 1799, too long after Pope's death to be unconditionally acceptable, but it is not improbable that Pope saw one of Macklin's many performances in the role. According to another anecdote, even later, Pope was so pleased with the revival that he queried Macklin on his research and was delighted to learn that Macklin adopted a red hat for Shylock because in his desire for accuracy he had discovered that Venetian Jews wore such hats.[23] Macklin is said to have believed that "Pope's" epigram implied a distinction between his production of Shakespeare's *The Merchant of Ven-ice* and Granville's *The Jew of Venice.*[24]

In the same year that Pope is reported to have watched Macklin's Shylock, he saw David Garrick as Richard III. In surprising modesty and humility, Garrick commented on the event:

When I was told . . . that POPE was in the house, I instantaneously felt a palpitation at my heart; a tumultuous, not a disagreeable, emo-tion in my mind. I was then in the prime of youth; and in the zenith of my theatrical ambition. It gave me particular pleasure that RICHARD was my character, when POPE was to see, and hear me. As I opened the part, I saw our little poetical hero, dressed in black; seated in a side-box near the stage; and viewing me with a serious, and earnest attention. His look shot, and thrilled, like lightning through my frame; and I had some hesitation in proceeding, from anxiety, and from joy. As RICHARD gradually blazed forth, the house was in a roar of applause, and the conspiring hand of POPE shadowed me with laurels.[25]

And to Lord Orrery, who had accompanied him to Goodman's Fields, Pope is said to have remarked, "That young man never had his *equal* as an actor, and he never will have a rival."[26] To Garrick's ears this was welcome praise, not, for once, merely a sop to his vanity, and within a year he wrote boastfully to his brother Peter that he expected to meet and sup with Pope.[27] In view of this mutual esteem, it is amusing to recall that one of Pope's most stinging lines on actors was said to have been used by Samuel Johnson to discredit Garrick. When Garrick was proposed for membership in the Literary Club, Johnson, re-membering Pope's *Epistle to Bathurst* (*Moral Essay III*), ex-claimed, "If he *does* apply . . . I'll black-ball him . . . Why, Sir, I love my little David dearly, better than any of his flat-terers do, but surely one ought to sit in a society like ours

Unelbow'd by gamester, pimp, or play'r."[28]

Pope's appreciation of Garrick's performance is a signifi-cant response to the art of acting. Over the decades acting tech-niques were becoming progressively naturalistic, and Garrick's method, adapted from Macklin, represented a considerable ad-vance beyond Betterton's. Pope, watching Garrick in one of his greatest parts, understood and admired the new approach. With his customary largeness of mind, he discerned that the old days of Betterton's supremacy, and of his own youth, were not necessarily the best. He might have been pleased to know that fifteen years after his death Thomas Wilkes could think of no better piece of advice to impart to the players than "First follow Nature, and your judgment frame / By her just standard, which is still the same."[29]

Pope spared the managers no more than the actors, for they too were part of what he treated as a conspiracy to undermine the stage. By offering difficulties to his many playwright friends and truckling to the popular demand for harlequinades, they revealed where their true interests lay. In an earlier age the king had singled out gentlemen of the stamp of Davenant and Killigrew to stage dramatic works of the highest quality, but the successors to the royal patentees were motivated by the hope of profits, not the desire to advance the taste of the public. Moreover, since many of the eighteenth-century managers had been actors before reaching managerial status, they could be attacked on several fronts. It is not likely that Pope wrote of John Rich or the Cibbers, father and son, without recalling that they served in a dual capacity. Yet when he denounced managers, Pope aimed primarily at their commercialism and the deceitfulness and disgusting manners which reflected it. From observing such outrageous behavior as that displayed by Colley Cibber before Fenton and by Fleetwood before Hill, he had learned that plays which he recognized as excellent were almost sure to go neglected. As early as 1709 Pope was aware of the managers' duplicity and arrogance, when he wrote to Cromwell on the disruptive tactics of Christopher Rich which had caused the temporary closing of Drury Lane:

The afflicted Subjects of France do not . . . so grievously deplore the Obstinacy of their arbitrary monarch; as do these perishing People of Drury, the Obdurate Heart of that Pharaoh, Rich, who like him, disdains all Proposalls of Peace, & Accommodation! Several Libells have secretly been affix'd to the great Gates of his Imperial Palace in Bridges Street; and a Memorial, representing the Distresses of these Persons, has been accidentally drop'd (as we are credibly in-form'd by a Person of Quality) out of his first Minister the Chief Box-keeper's Pocket; at a late Conference betwixt him and his first Minister about the part of the Confederates, & his Theatrical Majesty on his own part.[30]

Twenty-five years later Pope was still writing letters to Hill and Mallet on the same subject; nothing had changed but the names of the managers.

Nevertheless, Pope was always willing to make use of the managers on behalf of his friends. In baiting them as he did, he ran the risk that they might suddenly turn a deaf ear to his requests, for they were well aware of his contempt. Even so, within three years of the publication of the *Peri Bathous* and the *Dunciad*, in which the producers came under his fire, he made successful appeals to Booth and Wilks on Hill's behalf and to Rich and Cibber on Dodsley's. These victories, however, were not significant ones to Pope; almost as often as he made en-treaties to the managers, he professed to be out of contact with them.[31] The implication of all these transactions is that he con-sidered the managers good only for their usefulness to him.

The audience was as much to blame for the decline of serious drama as were the actors and managers—more, perhaps, since the professionals faced starvation if they did not please the crowds. Pope was sharp with the mob who came to the thea-tre to see sub-literary extravaganzas:

> There still remains to mortify a Wit,
> The many-headed Monster of the Pit:
> A sense-less, worth-less, and unhonour'd crowd;
> Who to disturb their betters mighty proud,
> Clatt'ring their sticks, before ten lines are spoke,
> Call for the Farce, the Bear, or the Black-joke.
> What dear delight to Britons Farce affords!
> Farce once the taste of Mobs, but now of Lords;
> (For Taste, eternal wanderer, now flies
> From heads to ears, and now from ears to eyes.)
> The Play stands still; damn action and discourse,
> Back fly the scenes, and enter foot and horse;

> Pageants on pageants, in long order drawn,
> Peers, Heralds, Bishops, Ermin, Gold, and Lawn;
> The Champion too! and, to complete the jest,
> Old Edward's Armour beams on Cibber's breast!
> With laughter sure Democritus had dy'd,
> Had he beheld an Audience gape so wide.
> Let Bear or Elephant be e'er so white,
> The people, sure, the people are the sight!
> Ah luckless Poet! stretch thy lungs and roar,
> That Bear or Elephant shall heed thee more;
> While all its throats the Gallery extends,
> And all the Thunder of the Pit ascends!
> Loud as the Wolves on Orcas' stormy steep,
> Howl to the roarings of the Northern deep.
> Such is the shout, the long-applauding note,
> At Quin's high plume, or Oldfield's petticoat,
> Or when from Court a birth-day suit bestow'd
> Sinks the lost Actor in the tawdry load.
> Booth enters—hark! the Universal Peal!
> "But has he spoken?" Not a syllable.
> "What shook the stage, and made the people stare?"
> Cato's long Wig, flowr'd gown, and lacquer'd chair.[32]

(Epistle to Augustus, ll. 304–37)

If such preposterous behavior was the worst sin of theatre-goers, it was not their only one. Some elements of the audience—specifically the upper classes—went to the theatre only to be seen. To them the stage provided nothing more than a social occasion. Pope did not omit them in his roll of offenders against taste. Although usually severe, when they happened to be friends of his he was gentle and teasing. Martha Blount, for example, was admonished not to be like one Pamela who "glares in *Balls*, *Front-boxes*, and the *Ring*, / A vain, unquiet, glitt'ring wretched Thing!"[33] The Blounts, however, were not willing to accept his advice, and in a few years Pope twitted poor Teresa for having to leave the pleasures of the town after the coronation of George I to return to the dreariness of country life. In town Teresa had enjoyed such frivolities as "Op'ra, park, assembly, play,"[34] but in the country she will have only early prayers and the visits of a dull parson. Perhaps Teresa, like

Clarissa of *The Rape of the Lock*, considered
ceive the bows of the side box and desired the (
of the "youthful Train" who, according to *T*
Fame, had a place at "Banquets, Balls, and Plays.

But the habits of vulgar and flighty persons v
ing matters. Pope, in his zeal to reform the age, .
regular attendance at the theatre was a sign of baseness. Persons of unequal rank shared boxes, thus upsetting the social
order, and London was crowded with skittish dolts who constantly dashed off to rehearsals.[36] If one wished to be polite to
such persons, one could speak only of "new Plays, / New Eunuchs, Harlequins, and Operas."[37] By linking plays with lesser
entertainments, Pope implied that all were equated in the minds
of the audience. Although these were persons whose goals
should have been higher than the satisfaction of rather vulgar
desires for excitement, there is no suggestion that any creature,
whether peeress or butler, listened to or cared for the intellectual content of the drama. The sole interest was in seeing
and being seen, and, though Pope wrote with the exaggeration
typical of his satire, he also wrote with conviction.

One may see in Pope's attitude the scorn of the aristocrat—
in Pope's case, the intellectual aristocrat—for those hapless
members of society who set themselves low standards. To a man
of his rank the encroachment upon the literary world of persons
marked by immoral behavior, greed, and ostentation could be
nothing less than outrageous. The juxtaposition in such poems
as the *Dunciad* and the *Imitations of Horace* of expressions of
fears for the theatre and for other literary genres makes sufficiently clear Pope's concern for his own interests. For if dramatic poetry was lost in the decline of popular taste, what was
the future of his own verse? On the other hand, he could not
have written so passionately on a subject not dear to him in its
own right. If the stage was to be saved, it was necessary to publicize the delinquency of its enemies.

VII

CRITIC OF THE DRAMA

To organize Pope's many remarks on the drama into a system of criticism is a difficult but obligatory task; difficult because they are scattered widely through his writings, obligatory because, when collected, they are an essential aid toward understanding the best informed taste of the early eighteenth century. What follows is a piecing together of Pope's random comments, taken from his poems, his Preface to Shakespeare and other prose, and his correspondence. As a result of this process, which entails the comparison of statements made over a period of more than thirty years, Pope emerges as a consistent and logical, if not particularly inspiring, critic of the drama.

For Pope, no less than for critics in any age, the drama stood or fell on its ability to meet rigid standards of form, language, and theme. None of the three could be slighted, and none weighed less than the others. A review of Augustan drama as Pope saw it will reveal his interpretation of each.

Modern critics have been quick to perceive Pope's intense concern for matters of form. Despite his almost exclusive use of heroic couplets in lengthy series, a form which suggests collections of aphorisms, Pope's poems are closely designed. The attention to detail, the imitation of familiar genres, the careful use of transitional devices, and the establishment of unmistakable points of view (the "persona") for the sake of unity, all reveal Pope's patient and indefatigable care for the shape of his work. It is to be expected, therefore, that Pope should show the same attentiveness to form in the work of other writers, not excepting dramatists.

In the *Essay on Criticism,* almost the first of his major

poems, Pope gave evidence of his basic interest in form. In this work "nature" and the "rules" are equated, and there is no doubt that Pope's rules are Aristotle's. Addressing poets and critics alike, he admonishes:

> First follow nature, and your judgment frame
> By her just standard, which is still the same:
> Unerring nature, still divinely bright,
> One clear, unchanged, and universal light,
> Life, force, and beauty, must to all impart,
> At once the source, and end, and test of art.
>
> .   .   .   .
>
> Those rules of old discovered, not devised,
> Are nature still, but nature methodised;
> Nature, like liberty, is but restrained
> By the same laws which first herself ordained.[1]
>
> (ll. 68–73, 88–91)

Here nature is that which has universal appeal; it is unchanging, and whatever grows out of it or inheres in it is art. But nature is also regular—that is, whoever would re-create nature must not ignore certain basic rules. To complete the syllogism, then, art, which is the imitation of nature, must also obey the rules. What this means is that a literary work, if it is to possess universal appeal and significance, must have carefully controlled form. As a corollary, the implication is that a work *must* have moral significance to be considered art.

The *Essay* continues with Pope's expression of doubt that a work of art may be written according to any sort of master plan: "Some [critics] drily plain, without invention's aid, / Write dull receipts how poems may be made."[2] To follow the rules, then, does not alone guarantee success. The writer must have insight, judgment, and the knowledge of what he intends to do in his work. Later in the poem Pope makes clear that the poet must also be aware of the unity of his work. Parts must adhere to one another, to make up an intelligible whole; and the critic, when considering the finished work, must, in turn, be aware of the poet's intentions.[3] With an incident from the career of Don Quixote as an illustration, Pope reinforces the point with respect to the drama:

Once on a time, La Mancha's knight, they say,
A certain bard encount'ring on the way,
Discoursed in terms as just, with looks as sage,
As e'er could Dennis, of the Grecian stage;
Concluding all were desp'rate sots and fools,
Who durst depart from Aristotle's rules.
Our author, happy in a judge so nice,
Produced his play, and begged the knight's advice;
Made him observe the subject, and the plot,
The manners, passions, unities, what not,
All which, exact to rule, were brought about,
Were but a combat in the lists left out.
"What! leave the combat out!" exclaims the knight;
Yes, or we must renounce the Stagyrite.
"Not so, by heav'n!" he answers in a rage,
"Knights, squires, and steeds, must enter on the stage."
So vast a throng the stage can ne'er contain.
"Then build a new, or act it in a plain."
    Thus critics, of less judgment than caprice,
Curious not knowing, not exact but nice,
Form short ideas; and offend in arts
As most in manners, by a love to parts.[4]

(ll. 267–88)

Don Quixote is presented as a shortsighted and perverse critic who supports the rules until he learns that they will interfere with his pleasure. He wants the knights, the squires, the battle. On being told that the theatre can never stage so much commotion, he suggests a new and drastic procedure: put the play on outside, where there is plenty of room. In this attitude he is obviously unreasonable. His defense of the unities is only sham, since he so readily abandons it, and the playwright must take up the fight for regularity. Pope's position is clear enough: show in a theatre only what reason itself dictates is proper for presentation there. Since a battle cannot be staged successfully, it must not be staged at all. Moreover, a battle is not important: if the rules prevent the staging of a battle, it is not only inappropriate but insignificant. This is a kind of moral justification of unity of action.

How closely did Pope stick to these principles of form during his career? In *The Guardian* No. 78, June 10, 1713, "A Receipt to Make an Epick Poem," he ironically restated the point that works of art cannot be made to order. Yet later on when he received play after play from acquaintances who were attempting to do just that, he made no comment. In the plays of Hill, Thomson, and Mallet, not to mention the lesser personages who plagued him, one may look in vain for a single work of genius. The form was consistent, of course, with every play save the two satires by Dodsley composed in scrupulous compliance with the unities almost as though cut to conform to a pattern or, to use Pope's word, receipt. These were special cases, however, for they were the works of friends and therefore at least partially exempt from criticism. His disapproval of adaptations so often reaffirmed (except in criticism of the works of friends) is closely related to the same issue.

But in his Preface to Shakespeare, Pope could not blink at the problem of form, for here was a playwright whose technique differed drastically from neoclassical ideals and yet was profoundly significant. To present a logical argument upholding Shakespeare was not easy for Pope in the face of his training and convictions, but the urge to express his admiration was strong. A measure of his difficulty appears in the Preface which, though always sensible, is nevertheless an apology for Shakespeare and sometimes seems on the point of conflict with other statements of its author. Pope was confronted with the necessity of explaining to his readers that Shakespeare was a man of genius, but genius in a different guise from what their reading had led them to recognize as such. In a sense, he had to explain away those qualities which the Augustans took for Shakespeare's shortcomings: his utter unconcern for regularity, his loquacity, and his occasional vulgarity. It must be remembered that Pope and his contemporaries were accustomed to Shakespeare "improved" in adaptations of the plays to fit new standards of taste. Pope himself, for example, never saw any version of *Richard III* but Cibber's, even on the momentous occasion when he watched Garrick in the part; at no time did he have an opportunity to see *Antony and Cleopatra*, which had been entirely superseded by Dryden's *All for Love*, and he had been requested by Sheffield and Hill to give thought to their new versions of *Julius Caesar*. In order to prepare readers of 1725 for the original plays, it was first necessary to justify them.

It is worth noting that Pope in his Preface made no comparisons between the plays as Shakespeare wrote them and the plays as produced in Augustan London. As an editor, he had the "dull duty" to present an accurate text, with no errors or effacements—although he forgot his high purpose when editing at least one play, *Julius Caesar*. When the task called for concentration on a pure text (which, of course, Pope failed to deliver), it would have been unwise to bring into the discussion any description of the deliberately and markedly altered plays passing for Shakespeare in the London theatres. Pope therefore went straight to the heart of the matter with an apology for the form of the plays his subscribers were about to read: "The Poetry of *Shakespear* was Inspiration indeed: he is not so much an Imitator, as an Instrument, of Nature; and 'tis not so just to say that he speaks from her, as that she speaks thro' him."[5] Here is the perplexing word "nature" again, this time applied to the work of an "irregular" playwright. But Pope's meaning is clear: a clever rhetorician, he insists at this point that nature, or universal significance, *controls* the playwright so that he may later excuse the absence of the unities in the plays. If the playwright is the device and not the imitator, he is not obliged to copy nature in order to create works of art, for nature has simply made use of him without his being aware of her intervention in the process of his thought.

Pope then advances to the next position: Shakespeare knew nothing about Aristotle's rules, for he was not (Pope believed) a learned man. Indeed, Pope argues, it was Ben Jonson, not Shakespeare, who brought learning to the stage; but he too found it difficult to explain to the audience what he was doing. It is improper, therefore, to judge Shakespeare by the rules, since to do so "is like trying a man by the Laws of one Country, who acted under those of another."[6] This notion, incidentally, Pope took from Rowe, who had formulated it in nearly the same words in his brief life of Shakespeare: "But as *Shakespear* liv'd under a kind of mere Light of Nature, and had never been made acquainted with the Regularity of those written Precepts, so would it be hard to judge him of a Law he knew nothing of."⁷

Although he blamed the seventeenth-century editors for corrupting the plays, Pope attributed most of what he considered the intrusive material to Shakespeare himself. As he saw it, Shakespeare's predicament was in part that he was forced to please a vast and diverse audience. As an experienced player, Shakespeare knew what was sure to delight the populace, and he brought it into his plays at whatever cost to their integrity. Pope's opinion was, above all, aristocratic. He saw no reason to give even the slightest credit to the wishes of the pit: "Players are just such judges of what is *right*, as Taylors are of what is *graceful*. And in this view it will be but fair to allow, that most of our Author's faults are less to be ascribed to his wrong judgment as a Poet, than to his right judgment as a Player." The result of Shakespeare's catering to low tastes is that his plays are not flawless. Pope compared them to "an ancient majestick piece of *Gothick* Architecture," while the plays of his own time might be compared, he thought, to a "neat Modern Building." Despite the nobility of the Gothic building, it is bound to have "dark, odd, and uncouth passages."⁸ By inference, such blemishes were not to be encountered in neoclassical drama. The emphasis here is certainly upon the importance of form, and the point is that Shakespeare's plays are great in spite of their faulty construction. But Shakespeare, guided by nature, had no need to labor over form.

In view of this insistence upon regular form, it is not surprising to find that Pope's favorites among the other Renaissance playwrights were those whose work most closely resembled that of the neoclassicists. In conversation with Spence he gave high praise to Sackville and Norton's *Gorbuduc*, which was "written in a much purer stile than Shakespeare's was in several of his first plays." Webster, Marston, Gough [Spence's spelling is "Goff"], Kyd, and Massinger he listed as "tolerable writers of tragedy in Ben Johnson's time."⁹ Except for Webster's plays, which are panoramic in structure, the works of these writers were closely modeled on Seneca's tragedies. Pope's inclusion of Thomas Gough is a good example of his persistence in seeking out the kind of literature which he preferred, for Gough's classical tragedies, which are almost forgotten today, were not mentioned, so far as the present writer knows, in the dramatic criticism of Pope's period. Equally significant is Pope's use of the phrase, "Ben Johnson's time," the implication being that Pope instinctively named the age after a classicist. It is worth noting, too, that Pope made an index to the Jonson folio in his possession, possibly with the notion of preparing an edition, and also an index to the work of Beaumont and Fletcher.[10]

The parallel neoclassical movement of the French theatre also came under Pope's gaze, although his remarks on it are sparse. It will be remembered that he had read Voltaire's *Zaïre* before looking over Hill's adaptation of it. But aside from that play and the works of the great seventeenth-century playwrights, Corneille and Racine, little else is mentioned in his poems and correspondence. Coupled with this, his admonishments to English dramatists to cease translating continental plays suggests that he preferred the drama of his countrymen. No matter where he looked, however, it was "regular" drama that caught and held his eye.[11]

With this preference for neoclassical structure, which emphasizes the power of the unities to insure quality in a dramatic work, Pope usually underrated any dramatic experiment. When, for example, he read *The Beggar's Opera*, he could not predict success for Gay. Nor did he react favorably to *The Toy-Shop*, Dodsley's little afterpiece. Apparently Pope refused to believe that these new types of drama, which departed completely from the usual form, could catch the fancy of playgoers.

But his attitude toward these plays was considerably different from his attitude toward other "irregular" theatre-works. Although *The Beggar's Opera* and *The Toy-Shop* were unusual, they were not anti-intellectual. Pantomime and opera, however, were far different matters. These he could not condone on any grounds, for they provided senseless action and progressed contrary to all respectable notions of form. To Pope, the pantomimes of Rich were mere shows with almost no dramatic interest to sustain them. He devoted thirty-two lines of the *Dunciad* to these miraculous transformations, presenting for the reader most of Rich's spectacular devices.[12] Gorgons, dragons, fiends, and giants; a winged book; planets dancing in the air—Pope covered them all with enough gusto to suggest that he may have taken some curious pleasure in them himself, and certainly he piques the curiosity of the reader. But his point is unmistakable, whatever may have lain hidden in his mind: such presentations were driving serious drama out of the theatre. The populace, which had been responsible for much that was undesirable in Shakespeare, demanded its shows, and playwrights and managers, eager for fame and money, gave them what they wanted.

In 1737 Pope was still petulantly harping on the point; the *Epistle to Augustus* is yet another complaint against the non-thinkers in the audience, who must always have something grand to see, but who were deaf to the efforts of the playwrights to give them something to think about. Art, which is the result of adherence to the rules founded on nature, was lost on them. Moral significance was of no concern to the pleasure-loving crowd. They came to see Pinkethman stuff chickens down his throat; to see infantry and cavalry and entire state processions cross the stage; to see "Cato's long Wig, flowr'd gown, and lacquer'd chair," but not to hear his words.[13] In all this Pope consistently clung to the opinions he had set down in the *Essay on Criticism* twenty-six years before; like Quixote's battle, mere display did not belong in the theatre.

Pope found a similar foe to sense in opera. In 1738 he questioned the value of "a Box where Eunuchs sing":[14] a fairly mild remark but one hinting at his distaste for castrati. But in *Dunciad IV* he was much more severe. Opera is a harlot, foreign and clad in patchwork. She is "too pretty much to stand," and before long she will put the stage to sleep. Handel alone among the composers earns Pope's praise, for his music "borrows aid from Sense."[15] "Patchwork" is the key word in Pope's description; it suggests that opera, a combination of words, music, and scenic effects, is not true to any form.

Pope's unfavorable reactions to pantomime and opera were not, of course, all due to the formlessness of these two types of entertainment. His principal objection was to their lack of intelligible content. They presented pageantry and spectacle only, and made no sense. To see them was to hear meaningless words. From Pope's random remarks on all literature, not only the drama, it is obvious that one of his primary demands was that the art of language be used to communicate significant matter. In the *Essay on Criticism* he stressed the matching of sound to sense, and he supported this in his comments to Spence that he had always striven for the compatibility of sound and meaning.[16] But this correspondence could not guarantee good poetry any more than adherence to a pattern could—the writer must have something to say. Pope's oft-quoted phrase,

> True Wit is nature to advantage dressed;
> What oft was thought, but ne'er so well expressed . . .[17]
>
> (*Essay on Criticism*, ll. 297–98)

is no less valid for being familiar. Wit consists in universal principles developed in suitable language.[18] Studies of Pope's prosody have shown the care that he devoted to his metrics, always with the intention of embodying his ideas in the most suitable verse.[19] As one might expect, he looked for the same quality in the works of others.

He was most conscious of Shakespeare's use of language in all its manifestations—diction, dialogue, and set speeches. In the Preface to Shakespeare, Pope listed some of the pitfalls of banal language his author had had to skirt in pleasing the multitudes:

In *Tragedy*, nothing was so sure to *Surprize* and cause *Admiration*, as . . . the most exaggerated Thoughts; the most verbose and bombast Expression; the most pompous Rhymes, and thundering Versification. In Comedy, nothing was so sure to *please*, as mean buffoonry, vile ribaldry, and unmannerly jests of fools and clowns.[20]

Shakespeare rose above these pitfalls somehow, and this is one of Pope's most willingly given tributes to him. Even so, Pope found it necessary to correct some details of Shakespeare's language, and although he thought many of the errors resulted from the carelessness of the playhouse and printing office, a less Latinate age has proved him mistaken.

A modern study of those passages and scenes in Shakespeare that Pope marked with stars and inverted commas demonstrates that his great preference was for set speeches and descriptive language. Upon rare occasions he designated a piece of action as choice, but nearly always he favored those lines which were didactic and sententious over those lines which were to be heard as the accompaniment of action. Thus, for example, he enjoyed Polonius's advice to Laertes and Antony's funeral oration, two passages of superb rhetoric.[21] It is not to be denied that these and the other speeches that Pope admired are among Shakespeare's best, but they are not all of the best that one might find in Shakespeare today. Furthermore, it may be added that none of the marked passages, even the lines of Polonius, imitates human speech; they are not lines in which the happy or wretched hero speaks in such a tone as to indicate his emotions through the sound of his speech. How firmly grounded in neoclassical dramatic diction was Shakespeare's editor may be told from this particular oversight.

The dialogue that Pope professed to admire in the plays of his friends was no less cold. Never is the emotion of a character given force in his speech. Nor is it surprising that rant, the exact opposite of precision, in which the actor utters meaningless sound, is also absent from those plays. Usually Pope praised the language of his friends' works and what he did not praise he corrected. In all his dealings with contemporary playwrights, the search for the exact phrase, the perfect turn of diction, was never abandoned. But the justness of Pope's praise remains questionable. In the tragedies of modern writers, he wrote to Oxford in 1726, "one continued Sameness of Diction runs thro' all their characters; and our best Actors from hence have got the custom, of speaking constantly in a pompous elevated voice . . . In like manner our modern Poets preserve a painful Equality of Fustian, throughout their whole Epic or Tragic works . . ."[22] Pope's criticism in this letter is not difficult to fathom. He found that all characters in the plays spoke alike, that diction provided not individual characterization but one kind of speech for all the dramatis personae. Every line proceeds on a high level, and this is in part the fault of the actors, for they have been corrupted by the playwrights. But if by "fustian" Pope meant emotional diction or speech tending toward rant, the implication is that he found fault not with the coolness of the speeches but with any attempt at warmth. While he might regret that his friends could not devise dramatic language to fit the personalities of their characters, he does not suggest that their words need be imitative of human speech under emotional strain. The same note of remonstrance comes into his remarks on Lillo's *The London Merchant*, whose language he found too luxuriant.

From the foregoing discussion it is a direct step to the third and final issue confronting Pope in his search for theatre. If the poetry of Augustan drama is weak, why was it tolerated? The answer leads to the very center of neoclassical thought. Pope found the plays acceptable because of their moral significance. To the man of very high principles, theatricality could be sacrificed for didacticism. Moral significance, the dramatization of universal beliefs, *was* entertainment. In all the plays that Pope professed to admire, one idea is dominant: the need to control the emotions by reason, the lack of which is repeatedly illustrated by portrayals of the wretchedness of men who by abandoning themselves to passion have neglected their stations in the universe. That the general public did not share this enthusiasm of the men of letters for poetic justice is evident in the playhouse records. It is true that poetic justice applied to comedy as well, but there it took a different form. The great audience who visited the theatre to relieve its tensions by laughter was happy to find that justice in comedy meant rewards rather than punishments, or, at the worst, light rebukes. But to men of intellectual achievement (or pretension) the importance of strict morality is undeniable, as witnessed by the unblinking, automatic acceptance of its values by Hill and his fellow-playwrights and, pre-eminently, by Samuel Johnson, whose *Irene* is all that any neoclassicist could wish.

As Pope declared in the *Essay on Criticism*, the dramatic form created by the unities abetted the presentation of neoclassical values. Within the narrow frame constructed according to the rules, events were put into admirable order. In Hill's

Caesar, for example, so painstakingly criticized by Pope, attention never wanders from the hero and his problems. The distractions which day-to-day living forces upon a man's consciousness are allowed no place in Hill's scenes. His Brutus, unlike Shakespeare's, does not listen to the music of a faulty lute and does not hear twice that his wife is dead. Whereas Shakespeare's hero answers many of life's petty demands, Hill's never hears them. Hill required his Brutus only to confront the question of loyalty—albeit a great question—and nothing more. For the sake of art, or art as he understood it, Hill permitted no other interests to vitiate the force of his theme. Thus neoclassical tragedy neglected humanity for the sake of dramatic regularity and an austere presentation of moral values.

Subsidiary to the question of moral significance is Pope's high regard for pathos. On first thought, the cold intellectuality of neoclassical tragedy, which required an audience to suspend its disbelief indefinitely, appears irreconcilable to the conviction that the emotions ought to be brought into play. Yet in tragedy after tragedy throughout the Augustan age characters turn from happiness to despair, from joy to sorrow, as the goal they are nearing eludes them. Constant reversals of action were intended to tug at the sympathies of the audience. When he responded to requests for his opinions, Pope impressed upon the dramatists the need to render just such effects. The reader will recall his injunctions to Fenton to secure a prologue for *Mariamne* in which the theme was to be "beauty and virtue in distress." In the same spirit he praised a scene in Hill's *Caesar* between Caesar and Calpurnia in which "dignity is admirably reconciled with softness" and reminded Mallet that no poet can manage "the moving of the Passions" if he does not have the innate ability to do so. How does all this fit in with the idea of the dominance of reason? The answer is that an audience that senses the play of emotions and observes the fears and hopes of a character can the more easily comprehend the deplorable lack of self-control which the character has revealed. Thus viewed, the emotions support the primacy of the intellect.

The same sense of moral significance underlay Pope's appreciation of certain plays not cast in the neoclassical mold. Lillo's

The London Merchant, which appealed to him strongly, is a
work of obvious didacticism, even though relentlessly committed to the purpose of eliciting unreasonable pity for its hero.
Cibber's *The Careless Husband,* which Pope praised, is also
sentimental, but its value as a corrective of morals is undeniable.
It would appear that Pope in judging both these works valued
their themes above all else. In Shakespeare, too, he admired the
ability to sway the passions. "We are surpriz'd, the moment
we weep," Pope commented, "and yet upon reflection find the
passion so just, that we shou'd be surpriz'd if we had not wept,
and wept at that very moment."[23] Yet Pope was unwilling to
praise sentimentality for its own sake. He was quick to scoff
at the sentimentality with which Ambrose Philips, for example,
let his shepherds and shepherdesses speak.[24]

To review Pope's likes and dislikes in the theatre is to risk
disappointment that so much, if not all, of what he found enjoy-
able is insufferably dull today. Static, talky, unreal, the tragedies seldom leap off the page. Yet if we turn to comedy, which
Pope wrote but did not write much about, we can find a good
deal to amuse us. In conflict with the belief that Augustan
comedy was the domain of the insignificant and ephemeral is
the hard fact that it can be read today, whereas neoclassical
tragedy, though intended to convey ideas of universal importance, is usually too tedious to be endured for any reason. It
has been wisely observed that the Augustans did their best work
when they ignored the literary values of their age;[25] Gay,
Arbuthnot, and Pope's *Three Hours after Marriage* is a case
in point. But the writers of tragedy who aimed for total precision of statement in dramatic poetry denied their works all
humanity. Despite the truths inherent in their coldly didactic
lines, they could not find a sympathetic audience.

Yet, to blame Pope for his sufferance of neoclassical drama
is to take an advantage of him which he would not take of Shakespeare—that is, to judge him by the principles of an age quite
different from his own. Pope deserves the fair treatment he
gave, for he was as much a product of the eighteenth century as
Shakespeare had been of the Renaissance. Of the tragedies
written in his time none was better than those he praised, no

matter how feebly they may impress a twentieth-century mind. When all drama since the Restoration is reviewed, only Dryden's *All for Love*, by virtue of its poetry, stands in the first rank of tragedy. Pope chose as well as he could among his contemporaries, and his love for Shakespeare demonstrates that he knew where excellence might be found.

If Pope failed as a critic to improve the taste of his age, it was not through supporting intellectual drama over gaudy extravaganzas but through failing to realize that vital themes must be accommodated with great poetry if they are to succeed, and that they may be expressed in other forms than "regular" tragedy. This realization, however, could not be hoped of one so fixed as he in the theatrical and dramatic conventions of his time. Working with playwrights, adopting their materials for his poetry, filling the pages of his most accomplished works with harsh words for men and women who cheapened the stage, Pope demonstrated at every turn his thorough acceptance of the intellectual values of Augustan theatre and his willingness to fight for them. Although the fight, through which English letters gained some remarkable poems, was a good one, the enemy forces entrenched in the theatre could not be driven out by contempt. Fortunately for Pope, he did not live to see them nourish pantomime until it fattened into burlesque, starve tragedy until it dwindled into melodrama.

NOTES

NOTES TO CHAPTER I

1. Alexander Pope, *Poems*, Twickenham Edition, VI, 96 (London: Methuen, 1954), eds. Norman Ault and John Butt. Unless otherwise indicated, all citations of Pope's poetry are to the Twickenham Edition (London: Methuen, 1939–54), John Butt, gen. ed. Hereafter cited as *Poems*.

2. Joseph Spence, *Anecdotes, Observations, and Characters of Books and Men*, ed. S. W. Singer (London: W. H. Carpenter, 1820), p. 25.

3. *Ibid.*, p. 197.

4. Owen Ruffhead, *The Life of Alexander Pope* (London: C. Bathurst, *et al.*, 1769), p. 23.

5. Spence, p. 276.

6. Joseph Warton, *An Essay on the Genius and Writings of Pope*, 4th ed. (London: J. Dodsley, 1782), I, 307–8.

7. Alexander Pope, *Correspondence*, ed. George Sherburn (Oxford: Clarendon Press, 1956), I, 18–20. Hereafter cited as *Correspondence*.

8. Sir Richard Steele, *Correspondence*, ed. Rae Blanchard (Oxford: Clarendon Press, 1941), p. 49 (and Notes); *Poems*, VI, 35–36.

9. *Correspondence*, I, 136–37.

10. Alexander Pope, *Works*, eds. Whitwell Elwin and William John Courthope (London: John Murray, 1871–89), II, 70. Hereafter cited as "Elwin-Courthope."

11. *Correspondence*, I, 138.

12. Charles Gildon, *A New Rehearsal, or Bays the Younger* (London: J. Roberts, 1714), p. 48. Pope himself commented on this in the "Testimonies of Authors" which precedes the *Dunciad*.

13. Peter Smithers, *The Life of Joseph Addison* (Oxford: Clarendon Press, 1954), pp. 45, 246–52; Colley Cibber, *Apology for the Life of . . . Written by Himself*, ed. R. W. Lowe (London: John C. Nimmo, 1889), II, 128.

14. Samuel Johnson, *Lives of the English Poets*, ed. G. B. Hill (Oxford: Clarendon Press, 1905), II, 99; Spence, p. 46.

15. Robert W. Halsband, "Addison's *Cato* and Lady Mary Wortley Montagu," *PMLA*, LXV (1950), 1122–29.

16. Spence MS in possession of Mr. James M. Osborn.

17. Spence, *Anecdotes*, p. 196.

18. *Ibid.*, p. 151 (and Notes). The phrases in half-brackets are in the MS owned by Mr. Osborn but not published in Singer's edition.

19. *Correspondence*, I, 173.

20. Jonathan Swift, *Journal to Stella*, ed. Harold Williams (Oxford: Clarendon Press, 1948), II, 654.

21. Sir Richard Steele, Dedication to *The Drummer*, in Addison, *Works*, ed. Richard Hurd (London: Bohn, 1856), V, 152–53.

22. Spence, p. 46.

23. Quoted by George Sherburn, *The Early Career of Alexander Pope* (Oxford: Clarendon Press, 1934), p. 102.

24. *Correspondence*, I, 174–76.

25. Cibber, *Apology*, II, 131–33.

26. *Ibid.*, II, 137–38.

27. *Poems*, VI, 96.

28. *Correspondence*, I, 176. For commentary, see Norman Ault, *New Light on Pope* (London: Methuen, 1949), p. 137; Sherburn, *Early Career*, p. 124.

29. *Poems*, VI, 101 (and Notes).

30. John Dennis, *Critical Works*, ed. Edward Niles Hooker (Baltimore: Johns Hopkins University Press, 1939–43), II, 43.

31. *Ibid.*, II, 104.

32. Alexander Pope, *Prose Works, 1711–1720*, ed. Norman Ault (Oxford: Basil Blackwell, 1936), pp. 156–64.

33. *Poems*, VI, 99. For commentary, see Sherburn, *Early Career*, p. 124.

34. Ault, *New Light*, pp. 133–38.

35. *Poems*, VI, 113–14.

36. Charles Kerby-Miller, ed. *The Memoirs of Martinus Scriblerus* (New Haven: Yale University Press, 1950), *passim*.

37. Sherburn, *Early Career*, pp. 136–39.

38. John Gay, *Poetical Works*, ed. G. C. Faber (London: Oxford University Press, 1926), p. 339.

39. *Ibid.*, p. 359.

40. *Correspondence*, I, 282–83.

41. Kerby-Miller, pp. 43–44.

42. *Correspondence*, I, 288 (and Notes).

43. *A Complete Key to . . . The What D'ye Call It* (London: James Roberts, 1715), Preface.

44. Gay, *Poetical Works*, p. 350.

45. *Complete Key*, p. 16.

46. Dennis, *Critical Works*, II, 120, 417.

47. Spence, p. 348.

48. William Henry Irving, *John Gay, Favorite of the Wits* (Durham: Duke University Press, 1940), p. 108.

49. Kerby-Miller, pp. 43–45.

50. Cf. Thomas Burnet to George Duckett, January 8, 1717: "Pope is coming out with a Play, in which every one of our modern Poets are ridiculed; as soon as it appears, I shall let you have it." *The Letters of Thomas Burnet to George Duckett 1717–1722*, ed. D. N. Smith (Oxford: The Roxburghe Club, 1714), pp. 119–20.

51. John Gay, *Three Hours after Marriage* (London: Bernard Lintot, 1717), pp. 44–46.

52. *Ibid.*, p. 18.

53. Advertised in the *Post Boy* as published February 2, 1717. See George Sherburn, "The Fortunes and Misfortunes of *Three Hours after Marriage*," MP, XXIV (1926–27), 91.

54. E. Parker, *A Complete Key to the New Farce, Call'd Three Hours after Marriage* (London: E. Barrington, 1717), pp. 5–8.

55. Sherburn, "Fortunes and Misfortunes," pp. 94–95.

56. Pope, *Prose Works, 1711–1720*, pp. 265, 279, 282.

57. John Wilson Bowyer, *The Celebrated Mrs. Centlivre* (Durham: Duke University Press, 1952), pp. 205–6.

58. Sherburn, "Fortunes and Misfortunes," pp. 104–5.

59. Advertised in the *Evening Post* of that day.

60. Joseph Gay [*pseud.*], *The Confederates* (London: R. Burleigh, 1717), "To the Reader."

61. *Ibid.*, Prologue. Gay is the "Wit *that waited on her* Grace" because of his service as secretary to the Duchess of Monmouth.

62. *Ibid.*, p. 5.

63. *Ibid.*, p. 20.

64. *Ibid.*, pp. 25, 29.

65. Parker, p. 8.

66. Colley Cibber, *Dramatic Works* (London: J. Clarke *et al.*, 1760), III, 114.

67. *Poems*, IV, 243, *Sixth Epistle of the First Book of Horace, Imitated*, ll. 87–88.

68. *Correspondence*, I, 395; Spence, p. 202.

69. Colley Cibber, *A Letter from Mr. Cibber to Mr. Pope* (London: W. Lewis, 1742), pp. 18–19.

70. Charles Johnson, *The Sultaness* (London: W. Wilkins, 1717), Prologue.

71. *Poems*, VI, 154–55.

72. *Correspondence*, II, 135–36; also Pope to Broome, September 18, 1722, II, 134.

73. Warton, I, 70–71. On much slimmer evidence, Pope has been identified with two other ventures in opera, Handel's *Acis and Galatea* and *Esther* (*Poems*, VI, 216–17, 432–34).

74. *Correspondence*, II, 489.

75. William Ayre, *Memoirs of the Life and Writings of Alexander Pope* (London: the Author, 1745), II, 115–16.

76. Spence, pp. 145–59.

77. Ayre, II, 116.

78. Burnet, *Achilles Dissected: Being a Compleat Key of the Political Characters in that New Ballad Opera* (London: W. Mears, 1733), p. 4. Ault, *New Light*, pp. 207–21, argues that Pope supplied the Epilogue for *The Captives* and the Prologue for *Achilles*, but Butt, *Poems*, VI, 438, 457, declines to print these attributions.

79. See Douglas Grant, *James Thomson, Poet of 'The Seasons'* (London: Cresset Press, 1951), pp. 140–41.

80. Ruffhead, p. 508 (Notes).

NOTES TO CHAPTER II

1. On November 3, 1732, George Granville, Lord Lansdowne, asked Pope to look over a revised version of his comedy *The She-Gallants* (1695), republished as *Once a Lover, Always a Lover* (Pope, *Correspondence*, ed. Sherburn, III, 327–28). This play is not considered here, however, inasmuch as Granville had printed it before consulting Pope. In all probability Pope received many similar requests.

2. *Correspondence*, I, 203 (and Notes).

3. Pope, *Poems*, Twickenham Edition, IV, 100. Warton, *Essay on Pope*, II, 22, held that the phrase "Virgin Tragedy" may allude to Richard Barford's *The Virgin Queen* (1728), but there is no evidence for this.

4. Harry William Pedicord, *The Theatrical Public in the Time of Garrick* (New York: King's Crown Press, 1954), pp. 134–40, has shown that mid-century Drury Lane audiences decidedly preferred comedy. While the dates covered by Pedicord's survey (1747–76) are after Pope's time, the inferences to be drawn from the study hold good for the years of Pope's active interest in the theatre, for the changes in taste reflected in mid-century drama had occurred decades earlier.

5. *Correspondence*, II, 28.

6. *Ibid.*, II, 134.

7. *Ibid.*, II, 29.

8. *Ibid.*, II, 33.

9. *Ibid.*, II, 34.

10. *The Theatre*, No. 15, February 20, 1720.

11. Spence, *Anecdotes*, p. 302.

12. Theophilus Cibber [pseud.], *Lives of the Poets of Great Britain and Ireland to the Time of Dean Swift* (London: R. Griffiths, 1753), V, 244.

13. See *Poems*, VI, 154.

14. Pope, *Works*, ed. Elwin and Courthope, II, 38, 64, 80 (Notes).

15. Spence, p. 257.

16. John Sheffield, Duke of Buckingham, *Works* (London: J. Barber, 1723), I, 331–32.

17. *Correspondence*, II, 81, 117.

18. *Works of Shakespear*, ed. Pope (London: J. Tonson, 1725), V, 271; Sheffield, I, 319. Of the twelve pleonastic expressions of this type listed by E. A. Abbott, *Shakespearian Grammar* (London: Macmillan, 1870), p. 22, Pope alters six.

19. *Works of Shakespear*, V, 259; Sheffield, I, 296.

20. *Works of Shakespear*, V, 266; Sheffield, I, 307.

21. *Works of Shakespear*, V, 225; Sheffield, I, 234.

22. *Works of Shakespear*, V, 258–59 (and Notes); Sheffield, I, 294.

23. *Correspondence*, II, 105, 134.

24. *Ibid.*, II, 152.

25. *Ibid.*, II, 145.

26. Warton, I, 307 (Notes).

27. Johnson, *Lives of the Poets*, II, 260. Possibly Johnson got his information from Pope through Savage before the *Lives* were projected.

28. *Correspondence*, II, 370.

29. David Lewis, *Philip of Macedon* (London: J. Watts, 1727), "Dedication." The play was first performed on April 29, 1727.

NOTES TO CHAPTER III

1. Another political dramatist with whose work Pope has been identified is Benjamin Martyn, the author of *Timoleon*, an Opposition tragedy of 1730. The *DNB* attributes to Pope the "strokes on the subject of liberty" which won most of the applause on the first night. But a check of the *DNB*'s sources uncovers no relevant facts. As noted earlier, Joseph Warton remarked that Pope had once at-

tempted a play about Timoleon, the Corinthian hero, but there is no evidence that this was the collaboration with Martyn.

2. Johnson, *Lives of the Poets*, III, 288.

3. Pope, *Correspondence*, III, 86.

4. *Ibid.*, III, 65–66.

5. William Aikman to Sir John Clerk, January, 1730. Quoted by Grant, *James Thomson*, p. 85.

6. *Correspondence*, III, 158. Also see Pope, *Poems*, Twickenham Edition, IV, 122 (Notes).

7. *Correspondence*, III, 177.

8. David Mallet, *Works* (London: A. Millar, 1743), pp. 27–28, 78.

9. Alexander Pope and Jonathan Swift, *Miscellanies*, the Last Volume (London: Benjamin Motte, 1727), p. 26.

10. *Correspondence*, III, 164–72, 173–74, 176–77.

11. *Ibid.*, III, 200–1.

12. *A Collection of Letters* (London: W. Owen, 1751), p. 78; *Correspondence*, III, 229.

13. *Correspondence*, III, 230, 235.

14. Aaron Hill, *Works* (London: Printed for the Benefit of the Family, 1753), II, 205.

15. *Correspondence*, III, 234.

16. *Ibid.*, III, 253.

17. *Ibid.*, III, 259.

18. *Ibid.*, III, 253.

19. *Ibid.*, III, 346.

20. *Ibid.*, III, 370–71.

21. *Ibid.*, III, 392–93, 394–95.

22. Hill quickly followed up this triumph with *Alzire*, a second adaptation of Voltaire, which received nine performances at Lincoln's Inn Fields in June and July, 1736. Strangely, Pope and Hill did not correspond on the play, nor is it mentioned in any of Pope's extant letters.

23. Grant, pp. 140–41.

24. Cibber, *A Letter from Mr. Cibber to Mr. Pope*, pp. 42–43.

25. Grant, p. 164.

26. *Ibid.*, pp. 180–81.

27. James Thomson, *Works* (London: A. Millar, 1762), II, 156–57.

28. Grant, p. 185.

29. Theophilus Cibber [pseud.], *Lives of the Poets*, V, 210.

30. Johnson, *Lives of the Poets*, III, 291.

31. Charles Dibdin, *A Complete History of the Stage* (London: C. Dibdin, n.d.), V, 57.

32. Benjamin Victor, *Original Letters, Dramatic Pieces, and Poems* (London: T. Becket, 1776), II, 11.

33. Hill, *Works* (1753), I, 308–9 (not printed in full by Sherburn).

34. *Correspondence*, IV, 152.

35. Pope to Hill, September 12, 1738. *Correspondence*, IV, 127.

36. *Ibid.*, IV, 108.

37. *Ibid.*, IV, 110–11.

38. *Ibid.*, IV, 121–23, 126–27.

39. *Ibid.*, IV, 131–32.

40. *Ibid.*, IV, 132–33.

41. *Ibid.*, IV, 145–46, 151–52, 158–60, 161–62.

42. *Ibid.*, IV, 165–66.

43. Thomas Davies, *Memoirs of the Life of David Garrick* (London: the Author, 1780), II, 34.

44. *Correspondence*, IV, 166.

45. Grant, p. 188.

46. Davies, II, 34–35.

47. Thomas Whincop, *Scanderbeg* (London: W. Reeve, 1747), Preface.

NOTES TO CHAPTER IV

1. Spence, *Anecdotes*, p. 332.

2. *Ibid.*, pp. 170–71.

3. For Dryden echoes and allusions, see Pope, *Works*, ed. Elwin and Courthope, II, 38–39, 250, 365 (Notes), 367; III, 153 (Notes); IX, 68 (Notes); *Poems*, Twickenham Edition, II, 204 (Notes); III, i, 14 (Notes); IV, 199 (Notes).

4. *Poems*, IV, 219 (*First Epistle of the Second Book of Horace, Imitated*, ll. 280–81); Spence, p. 281.

5. *Poems*, IV, 201, l. 85; Spence, pp. 46, 160–61.

6. *Poems*, IV, 105, l. 138.

7. *Ibid.*, V, 185, l. 308 (and Notes).

8. Pope, *Correspondence*, III, 378.

9. *Poems*, IV, 201, l. 86.

10. *Correspondence*, II, 358.

11. *Poems*, II, 191.

12. *Ibid.*, II, 200.

13. *Ibid.*, II, 167, 177.

14. William Congreve, *Comedies*, ed. Bonamy Dobrée, World's Classics (Oxford: Oxford University Press, 1925), p. 236.

15. *Poems*, II, 183–84 (Notes).

16. *Ibid.*, VI, 37.

17. Johnson, *Lives of the Poets*, II, 69, relates that Rowe enjoyed himself to the full on the first night, although the rest of the audience was silent.

18. See Pope to Caryll, September 20, 1713. *Correspondence*, I, 190.

19. Charles Gildon, *A New Rehearsal* (London: J. Roberts, 1714), pp. 46–47.

20. *Ibid.*, pp. 65–66.

21. Spence, p. 174.

22. *Correspondence*, I, 211.

23. *Poems*, V, 45.

24. *Correspondence*, I, 288.

25. Pope and Swift, *Miscellanies*, the Last Volume, p. 41. Edna Leake Steeves, ed., *The Art of Sinking in Poetry* (New York: King's Crown Press, 1952), p. 145, points out that the correct reading of Rowe's line is "And so good Morning, good Master Lieutenant."

26. Ayre, *Memoirs of Pope*, I, 210. Pope disapproved of Banks's plays in general. See *Poems*, V, 280–81 (and Notes).

27. Pope, *Prose Works, 1711–1720* [p. 305].

28. *Correspondence*, II, 25; for the poem, see *Poems*, VI, 400.

29. *Poems*, II, 344.

30. Nathaniel Rowe, *Three Plays*, ed. J. R. Sutherland (London: Scholartis Press, 1929), p. 242.

31. *Poems*, II, 281 (and Notes); Sherburn, *Early Career*, p. 202.

32. Quoted by Sherburn, *Early Career*, pp. 144–45.

33. Ruffhead, *Life of Pope*, p. 291 (Notes).

34. *Correspondence*, II, 171.

35. *Ibid.*, I, 380. See also Elwin-Courthope, X, 261 (Notes).

36. Clarance Tracy, *The Artificial Bastard* (Cambridge: Harvard University Press, 1953), p. 143.

37. *Correspondence*, IV, 417–18.

38. *Ibid.*, III, 442–43.

39. Theophilus Cibber [pseud.], V, 339.

40. Spence, p. 215.

41. George Sherburn, "The *Dunciad*, Book IV," in *Studies in English, 1944* (Austin: University of Texas Press, 1945), pp. 179–82.

42. Henry Fielding, *Writings*, ed. W. E. Henley (London: William Heineman, 1903), VIII, 204.

43. *Ibid.*, IX, 7.

44. *Ibid.*, XI, 209.

45. *Poems*, IV, 301, ll. 41–44; 313, ll. 1–2 (and Notes).

46. *Ibid.*, V, 345.

47. Wilbur L. Cross, *The History of Henry Fielding* (New Haven: Yale University Press, 1918), I, 366.

NOTES TO CHAPTER V

1. For the theory that Theobald's source was a manuscript play by Shakespeare and Fletcher, see E. K. Chambers, *William Shakespeare* (Oxford: Clarendon Press, 1930), I, 539–42. I am grateful to Professor Gerald E. Bentley for calling Chambers's commentary to my attention. For Pope's view, see Pope to Hill, June 9, 1738, Pope, *Correspondence*, IV, 102.

2. Pope and Swift, *Miscellanies*, the Last Volume, pp. 26, 28, 31, 52, 70.

3. Cited by Steeves, ed. *The Art of Sinking in Poetry*, p. 139.

4. Pope, *Poems*, Twickenham Edition, V, xi–xii.

5. *Ibid.*, V, 93.

6. *Ibid.*, V, 87–88.

7. *Ibid.*, V, 180, l. 272 (and Notes).

8. R. F. Jones, *Lewis Theobald* (New York: Columbia University Press, 1919), pp. 24–30.

9. George Sherburn, ed. *The Best of Pope*, rev. ed. (New York: Ronald Press, 1940), p. 450.

10. *Poems*, V, 75, l.106; 176–80, ll. 229–72.

11. *Correspondence*, III, 357. Pope thought the play was titled "Secret Love or some such name."

12. Theobald is also mentioned in the prose *A Master Key to Popery* attributed to Pope (*Poems*, III, ii, 174).

13. Ault, *New Light*, pp. 298–307, urges that the basic cause of the feud was Cibber's indiscreet gossip after surprising Pope in a brothel in 1714 or 1715. Pope is supposed to have been chagrined to learn that Cibber could not keep quiet about the incident. But the passage in Ault's study should be read with caution, for the story did not come out until 1742, when Cibber first printed it in his *Letter*, pp. 47–49. No rumors had spread during the intervening years. It may be that Cibber fabricated the entire tale, as Pope claimed.

14. Ault, *New Light*, pp. 309–11.

15. Cibber recalled the fact in his *Letter from Mr. Cibber to*

Mr. Pope, pp. 24–28. Pope's comment appears in the *Dunciad*, *Poems*, V, 279 (Notes).

16. Pope to Charles Jervas, July 9, 1716, *Correspondence*, I, 347; to Robert Digby, March 31, 1718, I, 473.

17. *Poems*, V, 289, l. 253.

18. *Miscellanies*, the Last Volume, pp. 27, 64, 67.

19. *Ibid.*, the Last Volume, p. 86.

20. Pope was well aware that Cibber was among the contenders for the honor. In a *Grub-Street Journal* essay, "Of the Poet Laureate," included in the Appendix to the 1743 *Dunciad*, he ironically analyzed the qualifications of Cibber, Theobald, and Dennis. Of the three, Dennis appeared the most suitable. For the epigrams, see *Poems*, VI, 327.

21. *Ibid.*, IV, 7, l. 37; 100, l. 60 (see Notes); 123, l. 373; 175, l. 138; 221, l. 292; 279, l. 6.

22. Cibber, *Apology*, I, 21–22.

23. *Ibid.*, II, 179–81.

24. On *Polly*, see *The Craftsman*, No. 135, February 1, 1729.

25. *Poems*, V, 279 (and Notes).

26. *Ibid.*, V, 281 (Notes).

27. *Ibid.*, V, 283, ll. 187–88.

28. *Ibid.*, V, 302 (Notes).

29. *Ibid.*, V, 68, l. 68 (and Notes).

30. *Ibid.*, V, 91 (Notes).

31. Charles Johnson, *The Tragedy of Medea* (London: R. Francklin, 1731), Preface.

32. *Poems*, V, 165 (Notes).

33. *Ibid.*, V, 33–34.

34. *Miscellanies*, the Last Volume, pp. 164–65.

35. See F. W. Bateson, ed. *Poems*, III, ii, 67 (Notes).

36. *Poems*, IV, 97, l. 23 (and Notes).

NOTES TO CHAPTER VI

1. *Second Epistle of the Second Book of Horace*, in Pope, *Poems*, Twickenham Edition, IV, 221, l. 305.

2. Sherburn, *Early Career*, pp. 49–50.

3. Spence, *Anecdotes*, p. 293.

4. Henry St. John, Viscount Bolingbroke, *Works* (London: J. Johnson *et al.*, 1809), VI, 348.

5. Roswell Gray Ham, *Otway and Lee, Biography from a Baroque Age* (New Haven: Yale University Press, 1931), p. 85.

6. G. A. Aitken, ed. *The Tatler* (London: Duckworth, 1898), I, 16 (Notes).

7. None of the theatrical chroniclers has recorded the Christian name of this actress.

8. Pope, *Poems*, Twickenham Edition, VI, 129.

9. Pope, *Correspondence*, III, 232; *Poems*, IV, 205, l. 123.

10. *Poems*, III, ii, 34–35.

11. *Loc. cit.* (Notes). Also, Thomas Davies makes the identification in *Dramatic Miscellanies* (London: the Author, 1784), III, 436.

12. *Poems*, IV, 75, ll. 5–6.

13. Richard H. Barker, *Mr. Cibber of Drury Lane* (New York: Columbia University Press, 1939), pp. 165–93.

14. *Poems*, V, 161.

15. *Ibid.*, V, 286–87.

16. *Ibid.*, IV, 306, ll. 115–16.

17. *Ibid.*, IV, 220 (Notes), 221, l. 293.

18. Spence, p. 197.

19. Pope and Swift, *Miscellanies*, the Last Volume, pp. 90–91.

20. *Poems*, IV, 81.

21. Hester Lynch Thrale, *Thraliana*, ed. Katherine C. Balderston (Oxford: Clarendon Press, 1948), I, 237; Charles Wentworth Dilke, *The Papers of a Critic* (London: John Murray, 1875), I, 310–12.

22. James Thomas Kirkman, *Memoirs of the Life of Charles Macklin, Esq.* (n.p.: Lackington, Allen, 1799), I, 264.

23. William Cooke, *Memoirs of Charles Macklin, Comedian* (London: Asperne, 1804), pp. 94–95.

24. Kirkman, I, 265. See also Thomas Gilliland, *The Dramatic Mirror* (London: C. Chapple, 1808), I, 427, for another opinion.

25. Percival Stockdale, *Memoirs of the Life and Writings of . . . Written by Himself* (London: Longman *et al.*, 1809), II, 153.

26. *Ibid.*, II, 154. Mrs. Thrale, *Thraliana*, I, 132, thought it was to Garrick's *King Lear*, not his *Richard*, that Pope accompanied Orrery.

27. April 19, 1742, in David Garrick, *Pineapples of Finest Flavour*, ed. David M. Little (Cambridge: Harvard University Press, 1930), p. 30.

28. This was Mrs. Thrale's contribution to Johnsoniana, in *Letters from and to Samuel Johnson* (London: A. Strahan and T. Cadell, 1788), II, 387. It was, however, vehemently denied by Boswell,

Life of Samuel Johnson, ed. G. B. Hill and L. F. Powell (Oxford: Clarendon Press, 1934–1950), I, 481.

29. Thomas Wilkes, *A General View of the Stage* (London: J. Cooke, 1769), 171.

30. *Correspondence*, I, 71–72.

31. Pope to Mallet, November 1, 1729, *Correspondence*, III, 66; Pope to Hill, December 8, 1738, *ibid.*, IV, 151.

32. *Poems*, IV, 221–25.

33. *Epistle to Miss Blount, with the Works of Voiture*, in *Poems*, VI, 63, ll. 53–54.

34. *Epistle to Miss Blount, on her leaving the Town, after the Coronation*, in *Poems*, VI, 125, l. 13.

35. *Ibid.*, II, 196, l. 14; 265, ll. 375, 382.

36. *Epistle to Bathurst*, in *Poems*, III, ii, 102, l. 142; *Second Epistle of the Second Book of Horace, Imitated*, in *ibid.*, IV, 171, l. 97; *First Epistle of the First Book of Horace, Imitated*, in *ibid.*, IV, 209, ll. 172–73.

37. *Fourth Satire of Dr. John Donne*, in *Poems*, IV, 35, ll. 124–25.

NOTES TO CHAPTER VII

1. Pope, *Works*, eds. Elwin and Courthope, II, 37–39.

2. *Ibid.*, II, 40, ll. 114–15.

3. *Ibid.*, II, 48–49, ll. 233–66.

4. *Ibid.*, II, 49–50.

5. Pope, ed. *Works of Shakespear*, II, ii.

6. *Ibid.*, I, vi.

7. Nicholas Rowe, "Some Account of the Life of Mr. William Shakespear," in *Works of Shakespear*, ed. Rowe (London: Jacob Tonson, 1709), I, xxvi.

8. Pope, ed. *Works of Shakespear*, I, vii–viii, xxiii–xxiv.

9. Spence, *Anecdotes*, p. 21.

10. Austin Warren, "Pope and Ben Jonson," *MLN*, XLV (1930), 86–88; "Pope's Index to Beaumont and Fletcher," *MLN*, XLVI (1931), 515–17.

11. See Spence, p. 10; *First Epistle of the Second Book of Horace, Imitated*, in Pope, *Poems*, Twickenham Edition, IV, 219, l. 274; 227, l. 375; *Dunciad*, *Poems*, V, 288, l. 250. For references to Molière, see *Poems*, V, 279, l. 132 (and Notes); 289, l. 254 (and Notes).

12. *Poems*, V, 176–79, ll. 229–60.

13. *First Epistle of the Second Book of Horace, Imitated,* in *Poems,* IV, 221–25, ll. 304–37.

14. *First Epistle of the First Book of Horace, Imitated,* in *Poems,* IV, 287, l. 105.

15. *Ibid.,* V, 345–48, ll. 45–70. Sutherland believes Pope's praise to be directed at Handel's oratorios, not his operas, although there is nothing in the poem to support this view.

16. *Essay on Criticism,* in Elwin-Courthope, II, 53–57, ll. 337–83. In this famous passage Pope displays the tricks of his trade but warns critics against basing their judgments entirely upon the meters of verse; it is more important that "The sound must seem an Echo to the sense." See also Dean Tolle Mace, "Sound and Sense in Augustan Poetic Theory," *RES,* New Series, II (1951), 129–39.

17. Elwin-Courthope, II, 51.

18. Edward Niles Hooker, "Pope on Wit: the 'Essay on Criticism,' " in R. F. Jones *et al., The Seventeenth Century* (Stanford: Stanford University Press, 1951), pp. 244–46.

19. See Edith Sitwell, *Alexander Pope* (London: Faber and Faber, 1930), pp. 265–85; W. K. Wimsatt, Jr., "One Relation of Rhyme to Reason: Alexander Pope," *MLQ,* V (1944), 323–38.

20. Pope, ed., *Works of Shakespear,* I, v.

21. John Butt, *Pope's Taste in Shakespeare* (London: Shakespeare Association, 1936), *passim.*

22. Pope, *Correspondence,* II, 370.

23. Pope, ed., *Works of Shakespear,* I, iii.

24. *Guardian* No. 40, April 27, 1713.

25. Austin Warren, *Rage for Order* (Chicago: University of Chicago Press, 1948), pp. 37–42.

INDEX

A

Addison, Joseph, 16, 33, 72; his *Cato*, 1, 5–13, 18, 21, 34–35, 37, 95, 97

Aeschylus, 56

Anne, Queen, 17

Arbuthnot, Dr. John, 17, 22, 26–27, 29, 32, 118

Aristotle, 44–45, 107, 110

Aubert, Mrs., her *Harlequin Hydaspes*, 30

Ayre, William, 32, 73

B

Banks, John, 73

Barry, Elizabeth, 95–96

Beaumont, Sir Francis, 112

Bellenden, Madge, 28

Berkeley, George, 8

Betterton, Thomas, 2–3, 94–96, 101–2

Bicknell, Mrs., 27, 94–97

Blackmore, Sir Richard, 27

Blount, Martha, 4, 104

Blount, Teresa, 104–5

Boileau-Despréaux, Nicolas, his *Lutrin*, 71

Bolingbroke, Henry St. John, Viscount, 6, 9, 55, 59, 95; his *Essay the Fourth, Concerning Authority in Matters of Religion*, 96

Booth, Barton, 9, 52, 89, 97, 103

Breval, Capt. John Durant ("Joseph Gay," pseud.), his *The Confederates*, 25–30, 97

Brooke, Henry, his *Gustavus Vasa*, 60

Broome, William, 32–33, 37, 41–42, 68

Buckingham, George Villiers, 2d Duke of, his *The Rehearsal*, 29

Buckingham, John Sheffield, 6th Duke of, 42, 61; his *Essay on Poetry*, 39; plays: *The Tragedy of Julius Caesar*, 39–41, 43, 109–10; *The Tragedy of Marcus Brutus*, 31, 39

Buckingham, Katherine, Duchess of, 31

Buononcini, Giovanni, 31

Burlington, Richard Boyle, Earl of, 48

Burnet, Alexander, 32

C

Caroline, Queen, 49–51, 57

Caryll, John, 4, 6–8, 10–12, 15, 19, 34, 72

Centlivre, Susanna, 24–25, 92

Charke, Charlotte Cibber, 97–99

Chaucer, Geoffrey, 95

Cibber, Colley, 5–7, 21–25, 29, 42, 78–79, 84, 87, 93, 97, 102–3, his *A Letter from Mr. Cibber to Mr. Pope*, 56, 90; plays, 25, 27–28, 33, 73, 88–91, 118